Celebrate Jubilee and Justice!

A Workbook from the
Center of Concern

By Jane Deren, Ph.D.
Commentaries by
James E. Hug, S.J.

Acknowledgements

Our thanks to Teresita Gonzalez, Emily Hage, and Mark Torma for their invaluable assistance and contributions to this publication.

Selected materials were adapted from the educational resources developed by the following:

The Canadian Ecumenical Jubilee Initiative
The British Catholic Fund for Overseas Development (CAFOD)
The Irish Catholic Agency for World Development (TROCAIRE)

We are grateful for their creative leadership in educational outreach for justice.

We would also like to thank the Center of Concern staff and our colleagues in schools and parishes who provided insightful advice for shaping the final text of this publication.

Design and layout: Loretta Stepka

Table of Contents

This workbook is designed to be ready to use in classes and groups with minimal preparation time. The pages may be easily photocopied for distribution. Permission is granted for photocopying for use in classrooms or study groups only, not for any commercial purposes.

The six sections in this workbook are based on the call to Jubilee in the Book of Leviticus in the Old Testament and on the recent social justice teachings of the Catholic Church. The topics are:

- Introduction to a Jubilee World
- Let the Land Lie Fallow
- Forgive Debt
- Free Those in Slavery
- Restore Just Relations
- Celebrate

A background essay on these Jubilee elements in the modern world introduces each section.

Each section also has the following:

- A sheet of **Prayers and Reflections** to open and close the sessions;
- **Activities** to actively engage students/participants as they learn about the Church's perspective on social issues;
- **Action Suggestions**;
- Lists of **Resources** for further study and engagement with the issue.

Note: *The teacher/facilitator does not need any previous background in the issues presented.*

The materials are designed to be used in a flexible way. The teacher/facilitator can:

1. Use all the materials for a complete unit on Jubilee and Justice.

OR

2. Pick and choose which materials to use for a Jubilee and Justice unit.

OR

3. Integrate selected materials into other units of study.

The sections do not have to be used in the order presented, nor is it necessary to use all activities and suggestions. You may add, substitute or adapt prayers, activities, resources, etc.

Note: *Some pages (e.g. prayers and reflection, quizzes and case studies) are to be copied and distributed to participants; these will be marked by a symbol, (pictured), in the top corner. You may want to have participants keep these handouts in a special folder so they can save them for their own reference and so they can reflect back over what they have learned when they do the activities in the final Celebrate section. Other pages (e.g. directions for the activities, answer keys) are for the teacher/facilitator and do not have to be duplicated.*

Introduction to a Jubilee World

Introduction to a Jubilee World

"You shall have the trumpet sounded loud
You shall hallow the fiftieth year
You shall proclaim liberty throughout the land
It shall be a jubilee for you."

Leviticus 25:9-10

The word "Jubilee" appears in chapters 25 and 27 of Leviticus. Jubilee is a call for right relations among people and with God's creation. It is a call that is echoed elsewhere in the Hebrew scriptures and which is central to Jesus' ministry to "bring good news to the poor . . . to proclaim release to the captives and . . . to let the oppressed go free." (Luke 4:18). While the word "Jubilee" may not be a centerpiece of biblical writing, the concept of Jubilee is an absolutely central theme of our living faith.

Jubilee is an all-encompassing vision of social and ecological justice that calls for release from bondage, redistribution of wealth, and renewal of the earth. In the biblical tradition, it was the "Sabbath of Sabbath years," a time that occurred after every seventh Sabbath year, every "fiftieth year." At Jubilee, slaves were to be set free, debts were to be forgiven, wealth was to be equitably and generously shared among all, and the land was to be given rest from its labor.

In 1994, Pope John Paul II described Jubilee as an effort "meant to restore equality among all the children of Israel, offering new possibilities to families that had lost their property and even their personal freedom . . . The riches of creation were to be considered as a common good of the whole of humanity . . . The jubilee year was meant to restore this social justice." The Pope has proclaimed the year 2000 as a special Jubilee year, and he has emphasized that restoring social justice to the world is central to our observation of this Jubilee.

The Vision of Jubilee

Although no records remain detailing an actual Jubilee in the days of the Hebrew scriptures, there was hope in the ideal that Jubilee offered: the attainable ideal of a more equitable society. The Jubilee text was written in the sixth century BC, when the Israelites were in exile and in need of a hopeful vision. This is exactly what they were given with the Jubilee passage.

As the world approaches the third millennium, we are also in need of a hopeful vision. We are in a time and place so far removed from the time of Leviticus that the drawing of any comparison is difficult. We have pushed the limits of science and the boundaries of technology far beyond what was imagined fifty years ago, let alone in the time of the Israelites. We have created economies far more complex than any kingdom or empire. And yet as the year 2000 approaches, humanity is still faced with many problems that cry out for a Jubilee: the threat of environmental exhaustion, international debt, unjust working conditions, and poverty around the globe.

Jubilee Challenge In 2000

Does Jubilee set off a resonant chord in this society? In contrast to values we esteem without question (productivity and competition, solid financial systems, exclusive private property, equal opportunity for all and the work ethic), the Jubilee prescriptions do not seem realistic. At best they seem idealistic religious aspirations; at worst they are labeled "failed nonsense." Thoughtful, hard-headed business people and politicians find it easy to dismiss them.

This is a serious problem for the evangelization of our culture. Jesus came to bring Good News to the poor, freedom to captives, recovery of sight to the blind and to proclaim Jubilee. But that Jubilee may seem totally unrealistic in this 21st-century, globalizing world. We who have been entrusted with Jesus' mission here and now have a serious challenge.

We need to discern the solution together, looking for foundations for the Jubilee spirit in other deeply cherished values of our culture (or better, our cultures, since the U.S. is home to many cultures) and in the guidance of our Church. This workbook has been designed to aid in that process of discernment.

The Jubilee spirituality proclaimed by Jesus (Luke 4) and grounded in Leviticus 25 has five general challenges: let the land lie fallow; forgive debt; free those in slavery; restore just relations; celebrate. As you work through the sections in this book, you will be given information and activities to help you reflect on these elements as integral to the Jubilee.

The U.S. Bishops have stated in the recent text, *Everyday Christianity: To Hunger and Thirst for Justice*, that the Jubilee is an invitation for us to see our lives from a divine perspective. All that we are and all that we do, individually but also as a nation and a faith community, should be in accord with God's will for building a global family of justice, mercy, love, and peace. Join us in exploring ways to become Jubilee people.

James E. Hug, S.J.

OPENING PRAYER

Holy Spirit, most welcome guest of our hearts
Reveal to us the profound meaning of the
Great Jubilee
And prepare our hearts to celebrate it with faith,
In the hope that does not disappoint,
In the love which seeks nothing in return.

Spirit of consolation, unfailing source of joy
and peace,
Inspire solidarity with the poor,
Grant the weak the strength they need,
Pour out trust and hope upon those
experiencing trials,
Awaken in all hearts a commitment to a
better future.

Pope John Paul II, *Jubilee Prayer*

REFLECTIONS

Reflect on the following and consider what aspects of Jubilee emerge from these selections. What is the Church calling us to be and to do as we face a new millennium and prepare for the Church's Jubilee in the year 2000?

In the Roman Catholic tradition, a Holy year of Jubilee is a great religious event, a year of forgiveness of sins and also of the punishment due to sin, a year of reconciliation between adversaries, of conversion and reconciliation, and consequently of solidarity, hope, justice, commitment to serve God with joy and in peace with our brothers and sisters.

The origin of the Christian Jubilee goes back to Biblical times. The Law of Moses prescribed a special year for God's people : "You shall hallow the fiftieth year and proclaim the liberty throughout the land, to all its inhabitants." (Leviticus, 25: 10).

Introduction to a Jubilee World

The celebration of this year also included the restoration of just relationships, the forgiveness of debts, the liberation of slaves, and a Sabbath for the land and the people. In the New Testament, Jesus presents himself as the One who brings the old Jubilee to completion, because he has come to "preach the year of the Lord's favor."

Pontifical Jubilee 2000 Central Committee Bulletin

It must be said that a commitment to justice and peace, in a world like ours, marked by so many conflicts and intolerable social and economic injustices, is a necessary condition for the preparation and celebration of the Jubilee.

On the Coming of the Third Millennium,
Apostolic Letter of Pope John Paul II

The Jubilee of the Year 2000 should be that privileged moment when each person will find that extra strength needed to turn away from egoism in order to receive God's pardon in prayer and fasting and thus to live in full solidarity with all persons, especially solidarity with the poor. The Pope is asking every weary, worn out, tired, and, at times, discouraged Christian to become a contemporary of the Christ of the Gospel and to give new vigor and freshness to the Good News that excludes no one.

Cardinal Roger Etchegaray, President
of the Pontifical Jubilee 2000
Central Committee and President of the
Pontifical Council for Justice and Peace

The [Biblical] jubilee was a time to restore freedom and justice among people, to reestablish relationships of equality, to remedy the conditions that kept the people oppressed and to cancel debts. The jubilee was intended to relieve the burdens of the weak and give people an opportunity to start anew. There was a clear social message in the jubilee. The jubilee year was an invitation to the people to see their lives from a divine perspective: all that they were and all that they did should be in accord with God's will for building a community of justice, mercy, love, and peace. Like the Israelites in their time, Catholics today ought to see the coming Jubilee as a call to renewed practice of charity, pursuit of justice, welcome to the stranger, and new efforts to permit all to participate in the full life of the community.

National Conference of Catholic Bishops,
Everyday Christianity:
To Hunger and Thirst for Justice

CLOSING PRAYER

Gracious, Loving God,
We live in a world that aches for a new beginning.
We watch as the gap between rich and poor
grows ever wider.
We watch as children continue to die from hunger.
We watch as your Creation continues to be in peril.
In this time we seek your face, a face of compassion
and hope,
The promise of a new vision and a new beginning.

Inspire us with your Jubilee Spirit to new
possibilities and new realities.
Bless us with the energy to work for justice for all
your children.
Hearten us when the task wearies us,
Nourish us with a foretaste of your new creation.
Help us sing out with Jubilee hope and rejoice in
this special time. Amen.

Adapted from the
Canadian Ecumenical Jubilee Initiative

ACTIVITY 1:
IN A WORLD LIKE OURS

1. Divide into small groups, with one person designated as the group leader.

2. Give everyone a copy of the *In A World Like Ours Quiz* (sheet #A1).

3. Have the group leader read the questions one at a time; have the group discuss the possible answers, and then mark their answer on the quiz sheet. (Participants are not expected to know these statistics, but trying to guess and then learning the correct answers is a way to raise awareness of the problems of our world.)

4. After going through the entire quiz, give everyone the answer sheet (sheet #A2) and have the group members take turns reading the answers.

5. Ask the group participants to discuss what surprised them, why it surprised them, and then have them briefly share their discoveries and insights with the entire group.

AND

ACTIVITY 2:
WE ALL HAVE A DREAM

1. Divide into small groups. Hand out sheet #A3.

2. Ask each group to discuss the questions on sheet #A3. What do they hope for in their own lives in the next millennium, what do they hope for others in the world, and what are some of the connections between our individual futures and the futures of others? This last discussion can be brief because as they do the activities in each section in this workbook they will get more ideas about connections between their choices and others' well-being.

Even for a brief discussion, you may have to guide the groups to think about how individuals are linked in this global society and how our lives can have positive or negative impacts on the poor in this country and around the world—and how the lives of those in Africa, India, or Latin America can have a positive or negative impact on ours (for example, hunger can cause developmental problems in a child who otherwise might have the potential to be a researcher and contribute to a cure for cancer.)

AND

ACTIVITY 3:
STEPS TOWARD A JUBILEE WORLD

1. Sheet #A4 has a number of quotes that speak to the Church's concern for specific aspects of social justice and the aspects of a world where Jubilee is taken seriously. Ask participants, in small groups, to go over the quotes and discuss the final question. You can have participants reflect on the ending question through journaling before a discussion.

2. Inform the group participants that in the next sessions you will be going into these aspects of a Jubilee world in more detail. Invite them to comment on what they have learned so far about the Church's commitment to social change as a part of its mission and its Jubilee celebration. Is this surprising to them? Why?

How does this new knowledge offer a new perspective of the importance of a Jubilee celebration at the beginning of the next millennium?

End all activity sessions with a closing prayer (see first page of this section), and continue to end this way as you go through all the sessions and activities in this workbook.

It must be said that a commitment to justice and peace, in a world like ours, marked by so many conflicts and intolerable social and economic injustices, is a necessary condition for the preparation and celebration of the Jubilee.

On the Coming of the Third Millennium,
Apostolic Letter of Pope John Paul II

Quiz:
In A World Like Ours

1. To provide basic education for all children in developing countries, it would cost $6 billion dollars more than is spent currently; in the U.S, we spend $8 billion dollars a year on cosmetics.
    T or F

2. To provide basic health and nutrition for all in developing countries, it would cost $13 billion dollars more than is spent currently; $17 billion a year is spent on pet food in the U.S. and Europe.
    T or F

3. Military spending in the world is _____ billion per year.

4. _____ billion per year is spent on advertising throughout the world.

5. The wealth of the world's 225 richest people is equal to _____% of the world's total income, while the poorest fifth of the world's population receive _____% of the world's total income.

6. If the debts owed by the governments of the poorest African countries were wiped out, the lives of 10 million children could be saved over the next ten years.
    T or F

7. One child born in New York City will consume, waste and pollute more in a lifetime than _____ children born in developing countries.

8. Because of poverty and discrimination in developing countries, _____ % more women than men are illiterate and female enrollment (even at the primary (K-12) level) is _____ % lower than male enrolment.

9. The world consumes six times more goods and services than it did in 1950, but over 1 billion people are still deprived of basic needs.
    T or F

10. The gap between health services for rich and poor is slowly closing.
    T or F

11. The United Nations has reported that extreme poverty in the world can be eliminated in the first half of the next millennium if 1% of the world's income could be used for basic services and development.
    T or F

Answers to Quiz

1. True.

2. True.

3. Military spending is $780 billion a year. The U.S. contributes to this figure not only by its own spending, but it ranks first in the world in the cost of weapons it sells to poor countries. (The U.S. ranks near the last of the developed countries in terms of the proportion of its resources it devotes to development of poor countries.)

4. $435 billion is spent on advertising in the world, nearly 8 times the amount that is now spent on development assistance to poor countries with hungry children.

5. The richest 225 persons in the world receive 50% of the world's total income, while the poorest fifth of the world —1.25 billion people — receive only 1.1% of the world's total income.

6. False. The lives of 20 million children could be saved by debt relief, which is why Pope John Paul II is calling on the World Bank and the International Monetary Fund to forgive the debts owed by the poorest countries. The Jubilee 2000 campaign is active in many countries, asking people of faith to sign petitions for debt forgiveness as an appropriate way to celebrate the Millennium.

7. The average American creates about 6 pounds of waste and garbage a day, more than 50 children do in developing countries.

8. 60%; 13%. Females of all ages suffer greatly under poverty.

9. True. If citizens can persuade their governments to support debt relief, to put more funds into development assistance, and pledge to reduce consumption and channel some of their funds spent on non-necessities to development and health agencies, we could witness the elimination of extreme poverty in one generation.

10. False. The gap between the health standards of the rich and poor is as wide as it was 50 years ago. Three out of four people in developing countries die before the age of 50, just as they did a half a century ago. 10 million children born in poverty this year will not live to see their first birthday because of lack of basic health care.

11. True. While the rich countries and individuals consumed $24 trillion in 1998 in products and services, the average African household consumes less than it did 25 years ago. The gap between the rich and the poor continues to grow, and the earth's resources continue to be used up by the rich; 20% of the world consumes 80% of the world's resources.

Source: The United Nations Development Program, *Human Development Report,* 1998

We All Have a Dream

We are invited to think beyond this life as we live it today and certainly beyond this century. We are invited to think and to hope beyond fixed parameters, beyond the doubts scattered in our paths, beyond those who think things will never change. We are invited to imagine a different world as we enter the next millennium.

(adapted from Doris Connelly,
"The Virtue of Hope")

1. Take a few minutes and imagine the positive kind of life you and your family would like to be living in the next millennium; consider your spiritual life as well as your lifestyle. Write down below some words that describe this future, or draw a symbol or picture that conveys your dream.

2. Imagine the kind of **positive** stories about the children (and their families) in the photos on the next page that you could be reading in newspapers and magazines or hearing on the news in the next millennium. Write down some **positive** headlines or the opening of some news reports that you may be reading or hearing in 10, 20, 30 or 40 years from now about these children.

"We are one human family: 'Love your neighbor' has global dimensions in an interdependent world. "

Pope John Paul II, *On Social Concerns*

"I know that the world does not change of itself. People with vision change the world because they are able to dream of another way of doing things than what we presently think of as the only course open to us. Slowly that vision can grow in the hearts and minds of people so that they yearn for a more just and loving world."

Archbishop Rembert G. Weakland, O.S.B.

3. Are there any possible connections or relationships between your own future and the future of the people in the photos? In the context of the quotes on this page, briefly discuss with your group any connections that you may have discovered.

World Jubilee to a Steps

■ Ethical consumption of goods and fair sharing of earth's resources

"In the moral order she bears a mission distinct from that of political authorities: the Church is concerned with the temporal aspects of the common good because they are ordered to the sovereign God, our ultimate end. She strives to inspire right attitudes with respect to earthly goods in socio-economic relationships."

"When we attend to the needs of those in want, we give them what is theirs, not ours. More than performing works of mercy we are paying a debt of justice."

Catechism of the Catholic Church

■ Respecting and enjoying the gifts of God's grace and of Creation

"Give us a pure and simple heart, that we may contemplate with ever renewed wonder your gifts."

Pope John Paul II,
Prayer for the First Year of Preparation for the Jubilee

■ Human beings and communities that are committed to joyfully praying and working for the common good of everyone in this global society.

"The Church rejoices in salvation, she invites everyone to rejoice, and she tries to create conditions to ensure the power of salvation may be shared by all."

Pope John Paul II,
On the Coming of the Third Millennium

■ Taking the Church's option for the poor seriously

"People living in poverty do not belong on the sidelines; they must be placed at the very center of our concerns."

Pope John Paul II, *On Social Concern*

■ Debt relief for the world's poorest countries

"The Jubilee is an appropriate time for reducing, if not canceling outright, the international debt which seriously threatens the future of many nations."

Pope John Paul II, *On the Coming of the Third Millennium*

■ Trade and investment policies that are fair to poorer countries; and agriculture and food policies that put people, not profits, first.

*"There must be solidarity among nations which are already politically interdependent. It is even more essential when it is a question of simulating the 'perverse mechanisms' that impede the development of the less advanced countries. In place of abusive if not usurious financial systems, **unequal commercial relations among nations**, and the arms race, there must be substituted a common effort to mobilize resources toward objectives of moral, cultural, and economic development, 'redefining the priorities and hierarchies of values.'"*

Catechism of the Catholic Church

■ Just labor policies for **all** workers in **all** parts of the world

"There is a need for ever new movements of solidarity of the workers and with the workers . . . the Church is firmly committed to this cause."

Pope John Paul II, *On Human Work*, 1981

■ Human Rights, both economic and social as well as political and civil, for all.

"The inalienable rights of every human person must be recognized and respected by civil society and political authority."

Catechism of the Catholic Church

Where are you on your journey of faith, which is both the journey inward toward a mature spirituality and the journey outward toward the involvement with social justice? How is the development of our faith limited without a sense of our call to be involved in the justice isssues of the world?

Reflection

The Gospel confers on each Christian the vocation to love God and neighbor in ways that bear fruit in the life of society. Real transformation of social structures begins with and is always accompanied by a conversion of the heart. As disciples of Christ each of us is called to a deep personal conversion and to "action on behalf of justice and participation in the transformation of the world." Holiness is not limited to the sanctuary or to moments of private prayer. Through their competency and by their activity, lay men and women have the vocation to bring the light of the Gospel to economic affairs, "so that the world may be filled with the Spirit of Christ and may more effectively attain its destiny in justice, in love and in peace." At times we will be called upon to say no to the cultural manifestations that emphasize values and aims that are selfish, wasteful and opposed to the Scriptures.

An Abbreviated Version of Economic Justice for All,
The U.S. Bishops' pastoral letter,
Catholic Social Teaching and the U.S. Economy

Action on behalf of justice and participation in the transformation of the world fully appear to us as a constitutive dimension of the preaching of the gospel… they call this justice an essential part 'of the Church's mission for the redemption of the human race and its liberation from every oppressive situation.

Synod of Bishops, *Justice in the World,* 1971

Our faith teaches that we have great dignity and worth as children of God. We must respect and commit to our own growth by a continuous journey inward and a journey outward, growing in concern, solidarity, and love for all members of the human family.

The Spirit of God is active in the world seeking fullness of life for all of God's people. The task before all people of faith is to discern where God's Spirit is laboring to bring a new creation into being and to join their efforts to that work of God. Such discernment calls for a conversion of heart and transformation of society, a reclaiming of values, and a renewed spirituality that revitalizes a sense of our own dignity and the dignity of every other person, our commitment to community, and our hope in the promise of New Heaven and a New Earth. Sustained by the story of the Gospel, and by the music, ritual, and common prayer of the liturgy, as well as careful reflection on and analysis of the new realities of a global society, such spirituality can unite men and women at the deepest levels of human experience. It can nurture a desire for solidarity that will awaken in each of us a special concern—a preferential option—for those caught in poverty, and transform our understanding of the good life to one of a life that is profoundly good for all.

Where are you on your journey of faith, which is both the journey inward toward a mature spirituality and the journey outward toward the involvement with social justice? How is the development of our faith limited without a sense of our call to be involved in teh justice issues of the world?

Suggestions For Action

1. Continue with the *Celebrate Jubilee and Justice!* sections on the following pages of this workbook.

2. Ask your class/group to take the U.S. Catholic Conference's Jubilee Pledge for Charity, Justice and Peace (see next page). Copy and distribute the pledge for participants to sign and recite together. Encourage others in your school, parish, and community to take the pledge. (For additional copies of the Pledge, you can also call 1-800-235-8722.)

3. Call or write the resources below to get on their current mailing list, in order to receive current updates about justice issues and activities. Mark your calendar to reserve reading and reflection time weekly to go over materials that are sent to you.

4. Pray and work to develop the virtue of hope: hope for the world, hope that you can live out your vocation as a Christian, using your talents and energy to help heal suffering, alleviate misery and poverty, and co-create a better world.

Resources

United States Catholic Conference
Social Development/World Peace
3211 Fourth Street NE
Washington, DC 20017-1194.
Tel: (202) 541-3000
Fax: (202) 541-3322
Web site: www.nccbuscc.org

NETWORK
801 Pennsylvania Ave. SE, Suite 460
Washington, DC 20003-2167
Tel: (202) 547-5556
Fax: (202) 547-5510
Web site: network@networklobby.org

Center of Concern
1225 Otis Street NE
Washington, DC 20017
Phone: (202) 635-2757
Fax: (202) 832-9494
Web site: www.coc.org/coc/
E-mail: coc@coc.org

Maryknoll Peace and Justice Office
P.O Box 29132
Washington, DC 20017
Tel: (202) 832-1780
Fax: (202) 832-5195
e-mail: mknolldc@igc.org

Jubilee Pledge for charity, justice, and peace

A CATHOLIC COMMITMENT FOR THE NEW MILLENNIUM

*The Jubilee of our Lord's birth calls us
"to bring glad tidings to the poor.
… to proclaim liberty to captives
and recovery of sight to the blind,
to let the oppressed go free."*

(Luke 4:18)

As disciples of Jesus in the new millennium, I/we pledge to:

PRAY regularly for greater justice and peace.

LEARN more about Catholic social teaching and this call to protect human life, stand with the poor, and care for creation.

REACH across boundaries of religion, race, ethnicity, gender, and disabling conditions.

LIVE justly in family life, school, work, the marketplace, and the political arena.

SERVE those who are poor and vulnerable, sharing more time and talent.

GIVE more generously to those in need at home and abroad.

ADVOCATE public policies that protect human life, promote human dignity, preserve God's creation, and build peace.

ENCOURAGE others to work for greater charity, justice, and peace.

Signature _____

Love for others, and in the first place love for the poor, in whom the Church sees Christ Himself, is made concrete in the promotion of justice.

Pope John Paul II,
On the Hundredth Anniversary of Rerum Novarum

WHAT IS THE JUBILEE PLEDGE?

THE JUBILEE PLEDGE for Charity, Justice, and Peace is offered by the Subcommittee on the Third Millennium and other communities of the National Conference of Catholic Bishops/United State Catholic Conference as an opportunity for Catholics to recommit themselves to serving the poor and working for justice and peace in the new millennium. As Pope John Paul has said, "indeed it must be said that a commitment to justice and peace … is a necessary condition for the preparation and celebration of the Jubilee." (*On the Coming of the Third Millennium,* no. 51).

For more information on how to fulfill your pledge, go to www.nccbuscc.org/jubileepledge.

Let The Land Lie Fallow

Let the Land Lie Fallow

The true value of our work in the world depends on our inner spiritual journey and the development of our spiritual life.

"Let the land lie fallow" can be interpreted both literally and figuratively. We must allow and help the environment to restore itself. To make that possible, we in the wealthy nations must begin simplifying our lifestyles and working to find sustainable patterns of living which will make it possible for all people on the planet to survive and thrive. In this culture, we also need to leave fallow time for personal deepening and for nurturing our family and community relationships.

By contrast, in the economy in which we each work daily for our living, that kind of attitude seems dangerous. "Productivity creates wealth." Progress comes precisely by exploiting our resources and adding value. We are urged to take advantage of every moment to do that, or our competition will pass us by. It is considered the genius of our system that competition drives constant improvement. And consumption is essential. Without rising consumption, economies around the world will stagnate or grind to a halt – and then everyone will suffer.

It is not necessary to deny these values of productivity and competition to embrace this dimension of Jubilee. It is only necessary to insist that they are not absolute. If we continue to push different planetary environmental systems beyond their ability to heal themselves, we know that we will destroy ourselves in the process. We will also violate the deep spiritual sense in our culture that reverences and glories in the beauty and power of nature. It is true that the global market system depends upon reliable, expanding consumption, but unless we find a way to make our consumption and development patterns environmentally and socially sustainable, the system will destroy creation.

We also should note that we must refuse, as a people, to let any single interpretation of "productivity" define the worth or dignity of a human person. It is a deeply rooted value in our culture to care for the young and the elderly, victims of natural and human tragedies, the needy and the handicapped; we consider it cruel to govern a society strictly by Darwinian laws of survival of the fittest.

Nor do we accept competition as the fundamental form of human relationship. Competition depends upon teamwork, and we have developed many legal protections in this country to guarantee that competition serves the well-being of the community.

Finally, we have learned from experience that just working harder and faster does not make us necessarily more competitive or successful. We need to work smarter as well. Working smarter requires enough psychic space to nurture creativity. Especially in this time of historical transition and globalization, our ability to contribute something truly healing and evangelizing for our culture and for the human community will depend upon our ability and willingness to step out of the constantly accelerating pace of our activities and systems to find a more contemplative and grounded space.

The true value of our work in the world depends on our inner spiritual journey and the development of our spiritual life. The activities on the following pages will help participants to consider the over-consumption in our society, to become familiar with Pope John Paul II's call to return to a spiritually enriching concept of the Sabbath, and to plan a time of retreat and renewal, Jubilee style.

James E. Hug, S.J.

Let The Land Lie Fallow

OPENING PRAYER

Slow us down, O Lord,
So we may "let the land lie fallow,"
So we may take the time
To view Your Creation with Reverence,
To see the needs of all Your family,
To share with our brothers and sisters,
To celebrate with them the abundant life You offer
As we create Jubilee time in our own lives
And in our communities.
Help us to become sensitive to
The rhythms of Your seasons
And to rest in the security
Of Your grace.

REFLECTIONS

The Sabbath—a time of rest, renewal, regeneration, and holiness—is a practice that speaks to the belief that all that is, whether it be land or ourselves as created beings, all belong to God. To create structures that speak otherwise is idolatry. Sabbath is the essential first step in the vocation of liberation, which is action based on contemplation, cessation of work and prayerful listening. Liberation and release from oppression comprise "the fast that God requires" (Isaiah 58:6). Jubilee is the vibrant weaving, made out of these two strands: Sabbath and Liberation. Jesus begins his ministry with this hopeful vision of Jubilee, and throughout his life lived Jubilee; his ministry is one of the places where the theory becomes practice.

> From The Canadian Ecumenical
> Jubilee Initiative, 1999

There is a fundamental expression and proposal of experiences in the Jubilee year — rest. Rest brings gift and relationship with God: everything is God's gift and we are able to refer everything to God. The culture of the Sabbath changes the quality of life; it leads one back to one's own roots, to the reasons for one's own existence, and can open one to the happiness of creation.

> From the Vatican's Jubilee 2000 Newsletter, 1998

Consider what the role of rest, contemplation, and "Sabbath time" has been in your life in the past and how it fits in your present life.

CLOSING PRAYERS

All shall be Amen and Alleluia.
We shall rest, and we shall see.
We shall see, and we shall know.
We shall know, and we shall love.
We shall love, and we shall share.
We shall share, and we shall praise.
All shall be Amen and Alleluia.

> St. Augustine

Lord, I am happy this day.
Birds and angels sing and I am exultant.
The universe and our hearts are open to your grace.
I feel my body and give thanks.
The sun is warm, and the sea splashes the shore.
I drink in your creation with my eyes.
I listen to the birds' jubilee with my ears.
Lord, I rejoice in your creation and your people.
and I rejoice that you call me to be a part of your loving family.
Bless this time, Bless your land and people.

> Prayer from Ghana

Activity 1:
The Consumer Lifestyle

Do the following in small groups if you have more than 8 to 10 participants/students.

1. Copy and distribute the pictures of families from around the world and the list of their possessions (sheets B1, B2, B3, B4, & B5). Ask group members to look at these carefully, noting the entire list of possessions for each family. Then ask them to imagine a photo of their family together with all they own displayed outside their home (this may have to be a wide-lens photo). Ask each participant to list, on the back of the photo sheets, as many of their own family's possessions as they can in 3 to 5 minutes (have them start with a specific room—their own room or the kitchen, for example).

2. Watch the clock and stop the writing after the allotted time. Then hand out sheet B6 with the drawing of a shopper who can't see that he is going over a cliff, with the quotes from John Paul II and related discussion questions. Designate a leader in each group to read the questions and invite discussion from the group. Allow 10-20 minutes for discussion and then ask for final comments from the entire group.

AND

Activity 2:
The Meaning of Sabbath Time

Copy and distribute sheet B7, which is readings from Pope John Paul II's Apostolic Letter, *The Day of the Lord*. Have participants read the sections and discuss the questions.

AND

Activity 3:
Simple Living, Jubilee Style

Copy and distribute the Simple Living, Jubilee Style retreat directions, sheet B8. Go over the directions with them, have them design, in small groups, a Jubilee retreat time and have each small group give a report on their final retreat program design.

Material World: A Global Family Portrait (Sierra Club Books) by Peter Menzel.

Family Possessions in Photo

(Roof, left to right)

- Mortars and pestles (3, for pounding grains)
- Sieves for sifting grain (2)
- Ritual cane (at roof edge)
- Musket (broken, inherited from father's father)
- Mosquito netting (covers bed)
- Bicycle
- Broken pot
- Basket (with clothes)
- Washing tubs (5, plastic and aluminum)
- Broken bark basket (with rags, scraps)

- Cooking pot (with ladle)
- Plastic water containers (2)
- Water kettles (2)
- Watering cans (2, one broken)
- Ceramic pots (5)
- Rectangular adobe brick mold (with sample brick)
- Battery-powered radio/cassette-tape player
- Folded blanket (between father and 1st wife)
- Sweet rice mush (near children, in cookpot fitted with firepot)
- Wooden condiment container
- Cultivating implements (hoes, shovel, knife, broad ax)

Material World: A Global Family Portrait (Sierra Club Books) by Peter Menzel.

Family Possessions in Photo

(Left to right)

• Wooden chair
• Jars (3, contain spices)
• Metal case (contains family papers, pictures, valuables)
• Ladder
• Wooden weights (4, used for wrestling practice)
• Print (on wall by weights)
• Bed (under family, used as couch during the day)
• Pictures of Hindu gods (2, being held by family)
• Firewood (to right of door)
• Bicycle (broken)
• Hindu print (hanging on bicycle)
• Metal pots (7), glasses (2), trays (4)
• Ceramic pots (2, behind metal pots)

• Basket of crockery (between metal and ceramic pots)
• Basket (with rice)
• Bags of rice (3, harvested last season)
• 2nd bed (leaning against wall)
• Blankets (3, draped on 2nd bed)

Family Possessions in Photo

(Foreground)

- Family bed (beneath family)
- Religious painting (held by father)

(Rear, from left to right)

- Sneakers (1 pair, high-top)
- Spinning wheel
- Plastic horse, plastic rooster, dolls (3)
- Large loom
- Finished fabric and family-woven shirts in traditional styles (hanging from large loom)
- Small loom with woven tablecloth
- Family house (adobe brick)
- Chair (in doorway)

- Machetes (3), sickle, shoulder bags (2), old calendar, religious pictures (6), hat (all hanging on house)
- Tables (3) with wooden trunk, small bowls, plastic flowers, Guatemalan flag, portable cassette-tape player
- Toilet (visible through bathroom doorway)
- Detached kitchen (adobe brick)
- Fuel supply (firewood)
- Axe (leaning against kitchen)
- Thermos, strainer, aluminum pan (hanging on kitchen)
- Red plastic wash basin, grill, plastic cups
- Clay firepot (beneath cups)
- Stone matate (for grinding corn to make tortillas)
- Wicker basket, clay bowls (4), ceramic pitcher
- Hoes (4)

Material World: A Global Family Portrait (Sierra Club Books) by Peter Menzel.

Family Possessions in Photo

(Foreground, left to right)

- Wheelbarrow (used by kids to play; occasionally to carry water)
- Bed (beneath 2nd daughter)
- Machete (held by father)
- Chairs (3, beneath parents, eldest daughter)
- Goat (held by youngest son)
- Saddle bags for donkey and bag of millet (behind goat)
- Toy VW bug (below goat, missing 4 wheels)
- Extra shoes (4 pairs)
- 2nd bed (old clothes used as mattress)
- Hoe and pestle (leaning on bed)

(Rear, left to right)

- Pantry cabinet with glasses (most with Coca-Cola logo), coffee mugs, trivet, plastic pitcher, plastic covers for food
- Storage hut for grain and clothes (raised to avoid rodents, ladder to enter)
- 3rd bed
- Chairs (2, one behind eldest son)
- Plastic washtub, wood and rope mop (leaning on chair)
- Horse, chicken and donkey with saddle
- Mortar (looks like tree stump) and pestle
- Plastic buckets (2, one inside the other)
- Plastic basket (green, in buckets)
- Tables (2)
- Crockery, coffeepot, oil lamp (on left table)
- Thermos, 4 felt hats (on right table)
- Chairs (2, boxes on them)
- Towel and dress (on chair to right of house)

Material World: A Global Family Portrait (Sierra Club Books) by Peter Menzel.

Family Possessions in Photo

(Clockwise from lower left)

- Donkey with saddle
- Butter churns (2)
- Hoes, rakes, other farm implements
- Dining table with 4 chairs
- Crockery, pepper grinder (on table)
- Storage cabinet for dishes
- Rooster (on top of storage cabinet)
- Containers used to wash dishes outside (against lower left corner of house)
- Garden trellis (left on hill behind house) not visible
- House (built by father) not visible
- Drying tobacco (hanging on front of house) not visible

- Barn for goats & chickens (visible behind house) not visible
- Goats (6) not visible
- Parent's bed
- Children's bedding (folded at head of bed)
- Cradle (currently not in use)
- Calf (tied to stake at bottom right)
- Extra shoes (1 pair - belongs to father)
- Rug
- Couch (family is sitting on it - doubles as children's bed)
- 2nd storage cabinet (directly behind family)
- Television
- Radio and youngest son's toys (on top of TV)
- Father's mandolin

Consuming

Pope John Paul II has said that "unless the resources and potential at any people's disposal is guided by a moral understanding, it can turn against these people to oppress them. Side by side with the miseries of underdevelopment, we find ourselves up against a form of super-development…which consists of an excessive availability of every kind of material good for some, makes people slaves of 'possessions' and of immediate gratification, with no other hope than the multiplication or continual replacement of things with something 'better.'"

Give some examples of people being "slaves of possessions."

Since we live on a planet that has limited resources, how does the "super-development" John Paul speaks of hinder the kind of human development where each person around the globe has the necessary basics to live a life of dignity?

People in the "developed" countries of the North, like the U.S., consume 80% of the world's resources, while many billions of people in "developing countries," in Africa and elsewhere, use 20%. What does this say about our values? How can these values be reordered?

Reading and Discussion on the Meaning of Sabbath in the Catholic Tradition

Reading From:
DIES DOMINI (The Day of the Lord), Apostolic Letter of Pope John Paul II

The theme of God's rest and the rest which God offered to the world is re-read in the New Testament in the light of the definitive "Sabbath rest" into which Christ Himself has entered by his Resurrection. The People of God are called into this same rest by persevering in Christ's example.

The day of the Lord is the day of new creation, linked with the Resurrection. It is also the day of Christian hope, therefore a day of celebration. (24,38)

The divine rest of the seventh day. . . speaks to God's lingering before creation. This is a "contemplative" gaze on creation. The rest decreed is an aid to help humans recognize . . . their calling to cooperate in the Lord's work and to receive God's grace. In honouring God's rest, humans fully discover themselves and are endowed with a kind of "fruitfulness," which deepens in men and women the joy of living and the desire to foster and communicate life. (63)

The Day of the Lord is a day of solidarity. St. Paul calls for a demanding **culture of sharing**, to be lived not only among the members of the community itself but also in society as a whole. (69,70)

Saint Ambrose addressed words of fire to the rich who presumed to fulfil their religious obligations by attending church without sharing their goods with the poor, and who perhaps even exploited them: "You who are rich, do you hear what the Lord God says: Yet you come into church not to give to the poor but to take instead." St. John Chrysostom is no less demanding: "Do you wish to honor the body of Christ. Do not pay him homage in the temple clad in silk only to neglect him outside where he suffers cold and nakedness. The One who said 'this is my body' is the same One who said: 'You saw me hungry and you gave me no food', and 'whatever you did to the least of my brothers you did also to me'. What good is it if the Eucharistic table is overloaded with golden chalices and a fellow human being is dying of hunger." (71)

These words remind the Christian community of the duty to make the Eucharist the place where fraternity becomes practical solidarity, where the last are first in the minds and hearts of the brethren, where Christ himself—through the generous sharing from the rich to the poor—may somehow prolong in time the miracle of the multiplication of the loaves. (71)

If the Day of the Lord is a day of joy, Christians should declare by their actual behavior that we cannot be happy on our own. (72)

The whole of the Lord's Day should become a great school of charity, justice and peace. The presence of the Risen Lord in the midst of his people becomes an undertaking of solidarity, a compelling force for inner renewal, an inspiration to change the structures of sin in which individuals, communities and at times entire peoples are entangled. Far from being an escape, the Christian Sabbath is a "prophecy" inscribed on time itself, a prophecy obliging the faithful to follow in the footsteps of One who came "to preach the good news to the poor, to proclaim release to captives and new sight to the blind, to set at liberty those who are oppressed and to proclaim the acceptable year of the Lord." (Luke 4:18-19) (73)

ACTIVITY 2:
WORLD CONFERENCE ON DEBT

1. Participants should be in groups of six to eight. Each participant will play one of the roles listed on sheet #C6. In these roles, they will take part in a global conference looking at possible solutions to the debt crisis. If they have not played the Get Rich Quick game above, the participants must first read background on the debt on Sheet #C4.

2. Give participants time to read the information sheets and consider the roles they will play. Give them about 20-30 minutes to hold their conference. Everyone must make an opening statement about their point of view and suggest a way to solve the debt problem for the world's poorest countries. Then they must discuss and debate the solutions.

CELEBRATE JUBILEE AND JUSTICE!
CENTER OF CONCERN

CLI CST

Session IV
pp. 45-48; directions 39-40

pp. 57-63

79-85; directions p. 73

CLI PSM

10 - 11
41 - 44
74 - 75
23 - 28

Discussion Questions

What messages do we get about rest, relaxation and celebration from the secular culture all around us? Think about images in advertisements and in popular television shows and movies: what experiences and lifestyles do they support?

How do these messages differ from Pope John Paul II's message about the importance of rest and celebration of a sabbath time?

What are the difficulties of responding to the Church's messages about the importance of a time of spiritual renewal while we are living in contemporary American culture?

What are some ways of dealing with these difficulties and putting more emphasis on sabbath time as a way to prepare for the Jubilee and to live in the Jubilee spirit?

Pope John Paul II states in section 10 of his Apostolic Letter *The Day of the Lord* that humans are called not only to inhabit creation, "but also to 'build' it and thus become God's 'co-worker'." What is the relationship between sabbath time and being God's co-worker in the contemporary world? How does sabbath time contribute to a different way of seeing the world and being present to Creation and to all members of the human family?

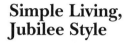

Simple Living, Jubilee Style

In preparation for the new millennium, create a model for a period of **Simple Living, Jubilee Style.** This can be a day, a weekend, a week, or a series of Sundays or weekends where you can "let the land lie fallow" by pulling back from your normal pace and style of living, to be open to God and Creation and to practice the spirituality of a simpler lifestyle. You may decide to use the model you create today for an activity together with the other members of your discussion group at a later time, or you may adapt the model you create in this session today for yourself, your family, and/or another group you are involved with.

Have members of the group read the following prayer out loud to set the tone for your reflections and planning

A Call to Prayer:
We who have lost our sense and our senses—our touch, our smell, our vision of who we are and who we could be; we who frantically force and press all things, without rest for body or spirit, hurting our earth and harming ourselves: we call a halt. We want to rest. We need to rest and allow the earth to rest. We need to reflect and to rediscover the Mystery that lives in us, that is the ground of every unique expression of life, the source that calls all things to communion.
We declare a Sabbath, a space of quiet, for simply being and letting be; for recovering the deep, discarded truths, for learning how to live again, in harmony with the earth and with all God's children.

From the United Nations' *Earth Sabbath*

Note: After you read each question, jot down some options to consider with your group. After you finish answering all the questions, give yourself some time to go back and see how some of the aspects of your retreat can be woven together. Have a group member take notes on your final decisions.

1. *The rush and pressure of modern life are a form, perhaps the most common form, of innate violence.*

Thomas Merton, *The Hidden Ground of Love*

Think about the rush and pressures of your life and what amount of contemplative time would be the minimum to begin to balance out the "violent" pace of our lives with a different rhythm. Decide with your group what period of time would be best to help you develop a deeper sense of Jubilee living: would a day, a weekend, a week, a series of Sundays or weekends, etc., be apropriate time for such a retreat?
Is there a special time during the liturgical seasons or in the months before January 1, 2000, when it would be meaningful to do this?
Revisit this decision when you have finished the other considerations, below.

2. *God of all the earth, giver of life and nurture, accompany our breaking of the bread of our lives.*

From: *Tales of the Heart*

Decide what you will—and will not—eat during your simple living time.
Will you have a time for fasting? And for feasting?
What kind of foods and drinks seem appropriate for a Simple Living retreat/renewal time?
What kinds of foods do not seem appropriate?
Where will you buy your food? (Are there local co-ops or small businesses in your community?)
How will you prepare and serve the food? How will you share the blessings of food with others, near and far?

3. *In and through the pain of our planet/we are called to make our Easter with the earth./ From collapse and devastation, we discover within the risen heart of the universe/cosmic peace, profound harmony...Pentecost for the planet.*

James Conlon, *A Canticle for Geo-Justice*

Decide how you will weave appreciation and concern for the environment into your Simple Living retreat/renewal time.
What are ways you can be attentive to and enjoy God's Creation?
How can you lessen pollution and waste during this time period?
How can you deepen your respect for the earth during this retreat learning more about the environmental problems we are facing and about how to be a part of the solutions?

4. *Ours is the religion of 'dwelling in the heart of God'*

Pope John Paul II,
On the Coming of the Third Millennium

Decide what kind of prayer time you want to experience.
How can you include silence, being aware of the presence of God, openness and listening to God's call, into your prayer time?
How will you balance community prayer with personal prayer and contemplative time?

5. *A more sane rhythm of life, then, is possible, one that meshes Sabbath and ministry, rather than the rhythm of desperate achievement and then escape.*

Abraham Heschel, *The Sabbath*

What kinds of sharing would "mesh Sabbath and ministry?"
What kind of sharing would be appropriate during your simple living time—what can you share and how can you share it?
How can you extend the sharing you normally do and develop a greater sensitivity beyond your normal community? What kind of sharing can you do with those in the poorest countries in the world?

6. *Notice and honor the radiance of/everything about you. . . Play in this universe. Tend all these shining things around you.*

Anne Hillman, "Prayer for Creation "

What activities are renewing and appropriate for this kind of Simple Living retreat/renewal time—and what kind of activities are not?
What kinds of activities bring real joy to you?
What kind of joyful activities enhance the human community and God's creation?
How can you balance activities involving others with joyful time alone with God?

7. *I don't want my children coming up to me and saying, "Now, what did you do about this suffering?" and my saying, "I didn't know about it."*

Dorothee Solle, in *Tales of the Heart*

How will you take some time to read and study about justice issues in our world?
What problems in our world do you want to learn more about?
(Suggestion: Your facilitator received, with these workshop materials, a copy of a report from the Center of Concern's and Archdiocese of Milwaukee's conference on Social Responsibility in the Age of Globalization, including a study guide. This is one way to go deeper into Catholic social teaching and the problems of the contemporary world.)

8. How can celebration be a part of all of the above? What kinds of celebration can you weave into your Simple Living, Jubilee Style retreat/renewal time?

Remember, "Like Jesus, we are called to a way of being in the world that deepens relationships, embodies and extends community, passes on the gift of life," so commit to putting at least some part of your planning into action.
When and how can you live out the call to live a simple life in the Jubilee spirit?

Suggestions For Action

1. Plan and carry out a retreat based on your reflections and discussions during the "Simple Living" Jubilee style activities.

2. Get a group together to read books on simple living and offer support to each other in changing lifestyles (a few titles are given below; they are available in most bookstores and on the Internet.).

3. Use the National Green Pages (see below) to check out the ratings before you make purchases so you can shop wisely.

4. Become more ecologically aware and involved through groups such as the ones noted in the resources below.

Resources

Advocacy Resources

Environmental Action Network
PO Box 7490
Boulder CO 80306-7490
Tel: (303) 444-0306
Web site: http://www.globalresponse.org

Books

DeGrote-Sorenson, Barbara and David Allen Sorenson. *'Tis a Gift to be Simple*, Augsburg Fortress Press 1992.

Durning, Alan Thein. *This Place on Earth : Home and the Practice of Permanence*. Sasquatch Books, 1997.

Menzel, Peter. *Material World: A Global Family Portrait*, Random House 1995.

Menzel, Peter, Faith D'Aluisio, Naomi Wolf. *Women in the Material World*, Random House 1996.

Periodicals

1999 National Green Pages. Updated annually. A directory of environmentally-friendly, socially-conscious businesses. $5.95 from Co-op America Tel: (202) 872-5307

Enough!, a quarterly report on consumption, quality of life and the environment. The Center for a New American Dream. 6930 Carroll Ave., Suite 900, Takoma Park, MD 20912.

More than Money, a quarterly magazine from More than Money 2244 Alder Street Eugene, OR 97405.

Too Much, a quarterly magazine. United for a Fair Economy and the Council on International and Public Affairs; 1-800-316-2739.

Forgive Debt

Forgive Debt

Lifting the debt burden of the poorest and most debt-ridden countries is essential if there are to be renewed efforts at providing basic necessities of food, health care, and education for their people.

"Forgive debt" has special resonance as we approach the Jubilee in 2000 because so many are in terrible poverty due to the debts their countries must pay, with ever growing interest, to the World Bank and the International Monetary Fund (IMF), and to developed countries such as the United States. Pope John Paul II has spoken out on this issue and has asked for debt to be canceled for the poorest countries around the world. Lifting the debt burden of the poorest and most debt-ridden countries is essential if there are to be renewed efforts at providing basic necessities of food, health care, and education for their people. The lifting of debt also provides one of the most powerful means to eliminate divisions among people and to end the subordination of some people to the desires and enrichment of others. To be in someone's debt is to be separated from and subordinated to that person. The same is true among nations.

To some, the argument against debt relief stresses that a reliable financial system is essential to everyone's well-being. Forgiving debts, they believe, may create a moral hazard: others will begin to expect that they too can borrow money and not have to repay it. The right of private property of the lenders will be violated. The incompetent and corrupt leaders that abused the loans in the first place will profit from the debt cancellation. Banks will not provide future loans to the nations that have been forgiven, so they will be starved of needed capital. Contracts will be undermined and trust in the system will erode.

But the risk of moral hazard must not be allowed to grow too large in our imaginations. In the U.S. economy, we have long provided the safety valve of bankruptcy court for those trapped in unpayable debts. If individuals and corporations can be relieved of difficult debt burdens in an orderly way that strengthens the system by providing a fresh start, the same can be achieved for debtor nations. There is a deep strain in the American psyche that supports such a move. It reaches out to the one who is down, who has made a mistake, who is the underdog—reaches out to offer another chance. In addition, the activity of forgiveness is an essential, ongoing process for Christians: we are called to forgive, to develop our own spirits, as well as to heal others.

We also know that all human governments can be corruptible, and they do not always act in their best interests. We know deep in our bones that it is wrong to press desperately poor people deeper into poverty because of the corruption or mistakes of their governments, governments they often had little power to influence or call to accountability. Our deeply-ingrained sense of fairness is violated when we recognize that large segments of poor nations' debt burdens were created by the oil crisis, the resulting global fluctuations in interest rates, and by irresponsible loans to corrupt governments of our Cold War allies.

The first activity of this section offers an experiential way of understanding why poor countries are in so much debt. The second encourages a role-playing debate to better understand the different perspectives, including the Catholic Church's, on the debt question. A Jubilee 2000 petition is also provided so participants can join with Catholics and faith-based people around the world to petition for debt forgiveness.

James E. Hug, S.J.

Forgive Debt

OPENING PRAYER

Liberating God,
We are inspired by the vision of Jubilee
To dream of a new beginning
Not only for ourselves,
But for our brothers and sisters around the globe
Who are sorely burdened
by the chains of debt.

Disturb, challenge and inspire us
As we seek to learn about their suffering.
Help us make the dream of debt forgiveness a reality.
Help us lift our voices in a cry for justice,
Convert to compassion those in power,
And bring healing to those without
Food, work, education, health care
Because of their country's debt.

Grant that we all may know
The Forgiveness of Jubilee
In all aspects of our lives.

REFLECTIONS

Christians will have to raise their voice on behalf of
all the poor of the world, proposing the Jubilee as
an appropriate time for reducing substantially, if
not canceling, the international debt which
seriously threatens the future of many nations.

Pope John Paul II,
On the Coming of the Third Millennium

International debt is something that is stifling
human freedom and has disastrous consequences
for our global family. Again, it seems, the poor are
providing for the rich. Indeed, the awesome
burden of international debt causes a loss of dignity
and hope for the poor, but also for all of us who
permit this.

Njongonkulu Ndungane, Archbishop of Cape Town,
South Africa, *Forgive Us Our Debts*

CLOSING PRAYER

O God, to whom we owe more than we can count,
In our desire to control all that is and will come to be,
We hold your other children
In the grip of debt which they cannot repay,
And we make them suffer the poverty we dread.
Do not hold us to our debts,
But unchain our fear,
That we may forgive
And release the Other
Into an open future of unbounded hope,
Through Christ our Savior. Amen.

Note: In order to provide an introduction to the international debt issue and the causes and effects of debt in poor countries, two role playing activities are given below. The Get Rich Quick Game has more complicated logistics, but it is an excellent way to learn how the debt crises came about. The second role play brings participants to a conference to debate what to do about international debt.

If you have time, both these activities are suggested. If this is not possible for your group/class, choose the one you think is most appropriate for your participants. We suggest you order the more comprehensive background resources on debt from *Jubilee 2000* and the *U.S. Catholic Conference* (see Resources list at the end of this section) so you have more information on this issue.

ACTIVITY 1:
GET RICH QUICK:
THE DYNAMICS OF DEBT

This game will take participants through five "years" of production in developing countries, as interest rates rise on loans and the price of exports drops, so they can experience how countries amassed unpayable debt. Read sheet #C1 with full directions for the game before you meet with participants and modify or expand as appropriate for your group (Note: this game has proven highly effective with participants in many different settings.)

Also, gather the necessary materials beforehand. For each small group you will need:
- An assortment of coloring pencils
- Ten or more copies of sheets #C2 and #C3 with the commodities of t-shirts, pineapples, and carrots outlined
- One land card (cut into four pieces)
- Between three and five $1 bills for each small group (you may use real money or paper money
- One pair of scissors
- One repayment card

Read over sheet #C1, with full directions for the game, before you meet with participants and modify or expand as appropriate for you group.

AND/OR

ACTIVITY 2:
WORLD CONFERENCE ON DEBT

1. Participants should be in groups of six to eight. Each participant will play one of the roles listed on sheet #C6. In these roles, they will take part in a global conference looking at possible solutions to the debt crisis. If they have not played the Get Rich Quick game above, the participants must first read background on the debt on Sheet #C4.

2. Give participants time to read the information sheets and consider the roles they will play. Give them about 20-30 minutes to hold their conference. Everyone must make an opening statement about their point of view and suggest a way to solve the debt problem for the world's poorest countries. Then they must discuss and debate the solutions.

3. At the end of the conference time, ask the group(s) to report what happened at their conference. Were they able to come to some agreement? Why? Why not? What did they learn about different points of view on this important international issue? What do they themselves think about the possible resolution to this problem?

4. Ask participants to follow the debate in the news media and through the web pages listed in the resource section to see what happens about the debt issue.

AND

ACTIVITY 3: JUBILEE PETITION

Hand out the Jubilee Petition (#C7). Ask your group if they want to sign the Petition. Brainstorm about how the petition can be widely circulated in your parish, school, community, etc. See suggestions for action for further follow-up.

Directions for Facilitating Get Rich Quick Game

1. Introducing the Game

Arrange your participants into groups. Hand out the materials to the groups. Give each group only one commodity to color.

Tell the groups: "The game you are about to play is a game of winners and losers. Each group represents a family living in a Third World country. The object of the game is to get rich quick using your available resources. Money is made by growing crops and selling them to the rich countries. This is done by coloring in carrots, pineapples or t-shirts (cotton) and cutting them out. The more shapes you produce the more money you make. Shapes must be colored in and cut out perfectly. No damaged goods will be accepted. Time is short since you only have 5 years in which to make your fortune. Every five minutes of the game represents 1 year. In the first year of production you will be given $1 for every two shapes which have been cut out and colored in correctly."

2. False Start

Start the game by saying: "On your marks, get set, GET RICH QUICK!" (*Hint: Some may rush to tear shapes with their fingers. Remind them that they will need scissors to make proper shapes.*)

Arrange a loan for scissors. Announce that each group can buy a pair of scissors for $15. Groups only have $3-$5, so suggest that they arrange a loan with you. Loans for $15 can be repaid over 5 years at $3 per year plus interest. Explain that interest is the money you charge for giving a loan. Interest in the first year will be $1. If asked, say that interest levels can go up or down. Hand out the repayment cards and have them signed.

3. Playing the Game

Start the game again by saying "On your marks, get set, GET RICH QUICK!"

You will stop the activity every "year" or 5 minutes and change the rules.

YEAR ONE: The sweet smell of success
In year one, give participants a taste of success—many poor countries had no problem repaying loans in the early years, the 1970s, when interest rates were quite low.

Stop the game after five minutes and ask for payments to be made (each group owes $3 + $1 interest). Add up how much each group has earned from their shapes. (Remember it is $1 for each commodity; do not deal in smaller amounts.) If they have earned more than the $4 they owe, give them the money they are due. Get a helper to record the amount paid by each group on their repayment card. Restart the game as soon as possible.

YEAR TWO: Overproduction reduces profits
In the early 1980's, poor countries saw the worldwide prices of their exports drop on international markets. After the next 5 minutes, stop the game. Each group owes you $3 + $1 interest.

Now change the price you give them for their shapes. Create tension between the groups by giving one or two of the commodities a particularly low price (e.g. $1 for 5 shapes) Give a reason for this ("People in the U.S. are off of pineapples this year;" "There are just too many carrots. . . the supermarkets just won't take them", or "Blue t-shirts are out of fashion this year," and tell them this actually happened with developing countries' resources in the 1980's).

Some groups might want to change their commodities at this stage. Let them do so but collect any half-colored sheets that they might have left over. This signifies the setback faced by poor countries as they plant new crops and wait for them to mature.

(*NOTE: Ensure that no group makes a profit this year. The most that any group should earn is $3, one dollar less than they owe.*)

YEAR THREE: Interest rates go through the roof This reflects the large rise in interest rates in the 1980s. Groups now have to repay $3 on their loan plus another $7 in interest. Give them a reason for high interest rates such as "I have to feed my family too!" Prices for shapes should be reduced further, e.g., $1 for every five to ten shapes. (*Hint: No groups should earn more than $2 for their shapes. If some groups are reluctant to part with the remainder of their savings offer to take a piece of their land as payment. Each quarter of their land is worth $5.*)

YEARS FOUR AND FIVE: More interest and fewer profits
Interest rates should be increased to $10 in year four, and $15 in year five. Commodity prices should be unpredictable and go up and down during these two five-minute "years." The most that any one group should earn for their shapes is $2, with some getting no money at all. Groups will have difficulty in making the last two repayments. If a group can't make any payment then mark $0 in the "Amount paid each year" column of their repayment card. You may also allow participants to sell land for a limited amount of money.

At the End of the Game:
Get each group to calculate the total amount that they have paid and the total amount they still owe. Get each group to compare these figures with the amount that they borrowed.

Debriefing: Ask groups to discuss how they felt about what happened in the game. Who were the winners, and who were the losers? Was it their fault that they fell into debt? What would have happened if the game had continued?

The difficulties that the groups faced are similar to those faced by consumers in the U.S. or in developing countries. Have the participants read Sheet #C4 and discuss.

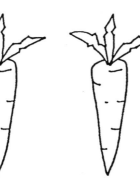

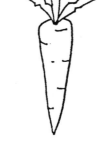

Repayment Card

Country:_____

You have borrowed $15 to pay for scissors

Year 1	Payment due each year	Amount paid each year	Amount owed
1	$3 + interest = $		
2	$3 + interest = $		
3	$3 + interest = $		
4	$3 + interest = $		
5	$3 + interest = $		
		Total amount paid $	Total amount still owed $

A Brief History of the Global Debt Crisis

Get rich quick! In the 1970's, Western banks had a great deal of money that had been deposited by oil producing countries. Banks were desperate to lend this money out quickly to avert a global financial crisis. They turned to Third World countries whose economies were doing well but who wanted money to maintain development and meet the rising costs of oil. Third World governments, good or bad, were encouraged to take the cheap loans at very low interest rates irrespective of what the money was being used for or their ability to repay.

Large and small improvements: The reason for these loans included the need to import technology (such as weapons, tractors, machinery, medical equipment) and large scale development projects (such as dams and bridges, which were sometimes political favors for anti-Communist dictators). Loans for development projects and imported technology were given as "aid" to the Third World, but in many cases 80% of this money was used to buy goods and services from the donor country.

Growing interest: Loans taken out in the 1970's were of an interest rate of about 6.5%. By the early 1980s the interest rate had risen to 19%. Many countries have paid back twice the amount that they originally borrowed, but they are now caught in the debt trap, spending all their valuable resources just to pay off the growing interest they owe.

SAPs: Since 1982, the International Monetary Fund and the World Bank (the two main international financial institutions) have been involved in lending money and refinancing debt in countries like Mexico which could not pay the interest on their loans. These new loans added to the debt burden and came with very strict conditions referred to as Structural Adjustment Programs (SAPs). SAPs force developing countries to cut domestic spending and gear their economy to export production so they can sell more outside of the country and thus raise funds for debt repayment. This has resulted in less spending on health, education and social services; privatization; layoffs in the public sector; cutbacks on food subsidies; and replacement of small subsistence farms with cash cropping for export. The poor in these countries have been hit hardest by such measures.

Plummeting profits: SAPS encouraged the developing countries to grow cash crops such as fruit, vegetables and cotton to meet their repayments. However, many countries were advised to grow similar crops and the resulting overproduction caused world commodity prices to plummet, significantly reducing their income. At the same time, the prices of essential imports from the West were increasing. These two conditions greatly contributed to the "debt trap". Unpredictable global markets and the low price of primary exports often meant that it cost more to produce coffee and cocoa than the crop could be sold for. As a result, many poor farmers switched to growing drugs in order to stabilize their income and support their families.

Land lost: As indebtedness has increased, more land in the Third World has been used to grow cash crops for sale as exports, not to feed local families. Millions of poor people have lost their land and flocked to the city in search of a better life; huge tracts of land have been sold to multinational companies to earn vital cash for indebted governments, and rainforests have been chopped down and sold to repay debts.

Unjust Relationships: Many poor countries will never be able to pay off their debts. They are entirely at the mercy of their creditors and can only be freed if the creditor country/bank gives its approval. Debt has also given creditors tremendous power to dictate the national policy of debtor governments. Debt, in the same way that slavery did, also provides Western consumers with a never-ending supply of cheap imports and cheap labor. Between 1981 and 1998 less developed countries paid over U.S. $2.9 trillion in interest and principal payments. This is double what they have received in new loans.

Limited Forgiveness: At the June 1999 meeting of the heads of state from Canada, France, Germany, Italy, Japan, the U.K., and the U.S. (the G-7) an agreement was reached to reduce some of the debt of impoverished countries, with qualifying restrictions. However, significant debt burdens remain in poor countries.

The Human Toll of Debt

Africa

In Uganda, the government spends (the equivalent of) $3.00 on health and education and $17.00 per person annually on debt repayments. One of every five Ugandan children dies from preventable disease before reaching the age of five.

While infant mortality rates rise in Zambia and 100,000 children die each year from diarrhea in Ethiopia, their governments spend four dollars on debt payments for every dollar spent on health for all children and adults.

Between 1990 and 1993, Mozambique was able to make only ten percent of its scheduled payments, adding $570 million to its debt. As a result of debt repayments, basic government services like health care and schooling have suffered dramatically.

Out of Mozambique's total (heavily indebted) population of between 16 and 18 million people, one million children do not attend primary schools, and each year 190,000 children die before their fifth birthday.

Latin America

Devastation from Hurricane Mitch is so great that it will take ten years for Honduras to recover. Meanwhile, the government continues to pay on its $4.1 billion debt, $147.7 million of which is owed directly to the U.S. government.

Nicaragua has the highest per capita debt in the world: each Nicaraguan owes six years of his or her income to foreign banks. In 1997 debt service repayments represented half the government's revenue, more than double its spending on health and education.

South America

Brazil is the world's largest deforester because it is one of the largest debtors, owing $200 billion. It is cutting 50,000 square km of rain forest every year for export to pay its debt.

Reflection & Discussion

"If you do good to those who do good to you, how can you claim any credit? Sinners do as much. If you lend to those from whom you expect repayment, what merit is there in it for you? Even sinners lend to sinners, expecting to be repaid in full. Love your enemy and do good; lend without expecting repayment. Then will your recompense be great."

Luke 6: 33-36, New American Bible

"You are not making a gift out of what is yours to the poor man, but you are giving him back what is his. You have been appropriating things that are meant to be for the common use of everyone. The earth belongs to everyone, not to the rich."

St. Ambrose

"I ask them to make a sincere effort to find a solution to the frightening problem of the international debt of the poorest nations ... An immediate and vigorous effort is needed, as we look to the year 2000, to ensure that the greatest possible number of nations will be able to extricate themselves from an intolerable situation."

Pope John Paul II, World Day of Peace Message, 1999

Consider the facts on debt above in relation to Christ's message, the words of St. Ambrose, and the words of Pope John Paul II. What does the Church call us to, and why is it difficult to respond? Is it surprising to you that one out of every four persons in Ireland signed the Jubilee 2000 petition? How can that happen in the U.S.?

World Conference on Debt

Roles:

A. Less Developed Country Minister

You represent a democratically elected government in a less developed country. Your country has been unbalanced by the burden of its debt. More is being spent on debt payments than on all of government services combined. Your people experience greater deprivation including inadequate nutrition, lack of access to health care and schooling, and escalating unemployment. Life expectancy has dropped to 46 years. You have defaulted on some debt payments already and do not know how long you will be able to keep paying on others.

B. Scandinavian Country Minister

You represent a First World country with a strong tradition of concern for the people in less developed countries. In recent decades, your country has provided some of the highest levels of overseas development assistance in the world. You have already canceled the Third World Debt held by your country, on a case by case basis. You believe that other First World countries and international financial institutions have the responsibility to follow suit.

C. Bishop from The Vatican

You represent the Vatican. Because of the Pope's pronouncements on the forgiveness of debts, you have a strong endorsement for the goals of the Jubilee 2000 campaign. You believe that there are strong biblical and moral imperatives to forgive the debt of the poorest countries.

D. Global Women's Organization Representative

You are representing a non-governmental organization concerned with women's issues. You believe that women and children are the worst victims of the debt crisis, and that their plight is being ignored. In highly indebted countries, you observe high rates of death during childbirth, many low birth weight babies, girls dropping out of school and few improvements in literacy.

E. Representative of the International Monetary Fund and the World Bank

You represent the International Monetary Fund and the World Bank. While recognizing that the global debt crisis presents a problem, you do not believe that the Jubilee 2000 campaign goals are an appropriate solution. You regard the others at the table as unsophisticated and somewhat naive. However, you are beginning to be concerned at the popularity of the Jubilee 2000 campaign. As guardians of the funds, you believe you have the information and ability to make the best decisions while keeping financial considerations in mind. While you find some arguments compelling, you are highly invested in keeping the Bank and Fund from changing quickly and giving up too much power.

F. Third World Farmer

You are a farmer with a family to support. Your country's debt affects you daily. The government has stopped subsidizing social services. That means you can't afford the children's increased school fees. Your brother's child died of malaria because he couldn't afford the hospital costs. Food and gasoline are beginning to cost more than you are able to earn. You have your land on which to grow food.

G. Representative of Non-Profit Advocacy Group

You have seen how debt leads to more poverty, conflict and refugees. You believe it also affects the global economy, as the Third World can't afford to buy much from the North. You think developing countries need to take some responsibility for the crisis. You want to negotiate the best realistic package for poor countries.

H. Rich Government Finance Minister

Your government is owed money by Third World countries. Because of public pressure, you are going to allow a limited amount of debt reduction; you don't want to forgive too much debt because it is contrary to the rule of law, it may cause instability in the global financial system and gives other countries the idea that they do not have to pay their debts to you.

The Jubilee 2000/ USA Campaign

222 East Capitol Street, NE
Washington, DC 20003-1036
Tel: 202-783-3566
Fax: 202-546-4468
Coord@j2000usa.org

For the latest info, log on to:
www.j2000usa.org

We Must Break the Chains of Debt!

We, the undersigned, believe that the start of the new millennium should be a time to give hope to people living in poverty. We must put behind us the mistakes made by both lenders and borrowers and *cancel definitively* the crushing international debt of impoverished countries burdened with high levels of human need and environmental distress.

We call upon the leaders of the richest countries, the commercial banks, the International Monetary Fund, regional development banks and other international financial institutions to write off these debts by the end of the year 2000.

We ask these leaders to cancel the debt in a way that benefits ordinary people and without conditions that perpetuate or deepen poverty and environmental degradation. We ask them to work with governments and civil society to prevent recurring cycles of destructive indebtedness.

Check here if you want to get more involved in the campaign ➝

Name (please print)	Address/City & State/Zip/Email	Signature	

Name (please print)	Address/City & State/Zip/Email	Signature	Check here if you want to get more involved in the campaign →
	--		
	--		
	--		
	--		
	--		
	--		
	--		
	--		
	--		
	--		
	--		
	--		
	--		
	--		
	--		
	--		→

1. Bring the Jubilee 2000 petition (#C7) to other individuals and groups in your school, church, community, and ask them to join Catholics and other faith-based people around the world by signing it. (For more information on the debt and the Jubilee 2000 campaign, see information below in resources.)

2. Write, call, email or fax your U.S. Congressional representative and your senators and urge them to take action on **significant** debt reduction for poor countries.

3. Learn more about campaigns that call for an end to structural adjustment programs that the World Bank and the International Monetary Fund impose on poor countries. (See below)

4. Learn more about campaigns to make international financial institutions more willing to share information on their decisions (more transparent), participatory in decision making, and accountable to the people and communities they were set up to serve. (See below)

Resources

Jubilee 2000/USA Education Packet
This education packet includes a wide range of educational resources on the issue of international debt.
  Contact: **Jubilee 2000/USA**
  222 East Capitol Street, NE
  Washington, DC 20003-1036
  Tel: (202) 783-3566
  Fax: (202) 546-4468
  Web site: www.j2000usa.org

Relieving Third World Debt: A Call for Co-responsibility, Justice, and Solidarity
The U.S. Bishops consider the impact of Third World debt on the poor. From the U.S. bishops' Administrative Board.
  Contact: **U.S. Catholic Conference**
  3211 Fourth Street NE
  Washington, DC 20017-1194
  Tel: 1-800-235-8722
  Fax: (202) 541-3322
  Web site: www.nccbuscc.org

Proclaim Jubilee: Break the Chains of Debt: Bread for the World's 1999 offering of letters kit focuses on debt and provides materials designed to help schools and parishes conduct an "offering of letters".
  Contact: **Bread for the World**
  1100 Wayne Avenue Suite 1000
  Silver Spring, MD 20910
  Tel: (301) 608-2400
      (800) 82-BREAD
  Fax: (301) 608-2401
  Web site: www.bread.org

Putting Life Before Debt: Produced in cooperation with the U.S. Catholic Conference, the International Cooperation for Development and Solidarity (CIDSE), and Caritas Internationalis, this statement offers an analysis of international debt from the perspective of Catholic social teaching.
  Contact: **Catholic Relief Services**
  209 West Fayette Street
  Baltimore, MD 21201-3443
  Tel: (410) 250-2220
  Fax: (410) 685-1635
  Web site: www.catholicrelief.org

Free Those
in Slavery

SECTION 4

The fact that "slave wages" may be better than no wages at all does not justify them. Nor does it make them acceptable to our deep-seated cultural sense of fairness.

The injunction to **"Free those in slavery"** challenges us to take a fresh look at the many causes of captivity in society. Around the world many millions of people are captives of migrant labor streams and sweatshops while a relatively small number of people become very rich from the labor of these "captives," and we in the industrial nations enjoy lower consumer prices.

In our culture, the right to profit often takes precedence over the basic human rights to food, shelter, and to jobs with safe conditions and decent wages, rights that the Popes have endorsed since *The Condition of Labor*, written by Pope Leo XIII in 1891. In the present economy, the laws of the market make demands, and there is ruthless and relentless competition for markets and market share. We are told that manufacturers must keep their labor costs down if they hope to succeed, that unrealistic labor demands drove factories out of this country in the first place. Besides, people in poor countries, they continue, are better off even with low-paying jobs than with no jobs at all.

One need not reject the right to profit to insist that current laws and policies can be improved and new laws and policies are needed to protect the rights of workers worldwide. The "laws" of the marketplace are not absolute or divine. This nation fought its bloodiest war to end slavery, and the first half of the twentieth century was marked by long, difficult struggles for safe working conditions and just wages.

The fact that "slave wages" may be better than no wages at all does not justify them. Nor does it make them acceptable to our deep-seated cultural sense of fairness. The anti-sweat-shop movement is gaining strength across the nation. Student movements on the nations' campuses are beginning to give voice to outrage that items bearing their university logo should be made under oppressive and exploitative labor conditions. We must be in the fore-front of the fight against contemporary forms of slavery, demanding justice for workers worldwide. Again, our own inner life and spiritual freedom are nourished when we take a stand against outer forms of slavery.

The first activity in this section will look at workers who are "enslaved" by unjust working conditions. A second activity allows participants to name and explore other kinds of slavery we see in the world and in our own lives. We are challenged to take part in our own libera-tion and the liberation of our sisters and brothers.

James E. Hug, S.J.

Free Those in Slavery

OPENING PRAYER

All the broken hearts shall rejoice;
All those who are heavy laden,
Whose eyes are tired at their work table
Shall be lifted up to meet with justice.
The worn out souls and bodies shall be healed;
Their hungry families shall be fed;
The imprisoned shall be free;
All earthly children shall regain joy
In the reign of the just and loving One,
Coming for you, coming for me,
Coming for all our brothers and sisters,
In this world, in this new time.

From South Korea

REFLECTIONS

Reflect on the following passages and discuss the Church's concern for workers.

Too often workers are reduced to being slaves to their own work, which is by no means justified by so-called economic laws. They should enjoy sufficient rest and compensation to cultivate their familial, cultural, social and religious life.

Second Vatican Council, *Pastoral Constitution on the Church in the Modern World*

Rich employers must not treat their workers as though they were slaves, but must recognize them as people who are their equals in personal dignity. What is truly shameful and inhuman is to misuse people as instruments for gain and to value them only as so much energy for production.

Pope Leo XIII, *The Condition of Labor*

CLOSING PRAYER

Light. Light a lamp for the sake of hope and liberation.
Hope and freedom sheltered in the heart will not be extinguished.
Do not be afraid. Be glad and rejoice.
The rain comes. Day comes.
The pastures are green again.
Trees dress with abundant fruit
Have hope. Hope is strength, staying power in the dark time.

Light. Light a lamp. Bring light to your own hearts.
Bring light to the people waiting for liberation.
A light of healing. A light of justice. A light of freedom.
Ready up all hearts.
The world of the past is gone. Creation is made new.
The love of God is come to dwell among us, to free us from sin and misery.
The fruit of love and peace is blossoming in our hearts and in our land.

ACTIVITY 1:
THE FACES AND FACTS BEHIND THE PRODUCT

Have your group look at the pictures on sheet #D1. The next sheets, #D2, D3, D4, D5, give the faces and facts behind these products. Divide participants so each product is assigned to a participant or to a small group. Have them read over the facts and make a brief presentation to the rest of the group(s).

How do the facts point to a form of slavery and bondage for the workers? Ask why we know so little about the faces and facts behind all the products we use daily. Read the case study on the students at Georgetown University (#D6). Since part of the Jubilee message is freeing people from all forms of slavery, discuss how your group can make some kind of difference in the Jubilee year. Ask for suggestions from the groups, read the Suggestions for Action, and then decide on at least one course of action.

AND

ACTIVITY 2: DIFFERENT FORMS OF SLAVERY

Copy and hand out sheet #D7. Read the opening passages, do an initial reading of all the questions and then have your group discuss these questions. (Appoint a group leader to move the discussion from one question to the next in a timely fashion.) Have the groups report to the entire class or gathering when everyone has finished.

WHO ARE THE **faces** behind the **PRODUCTS?**

Wal-Mart Worker

Banana Picker

Strawberry Worker

Nike Shoe Factory

Bananas

Facts:

Plantation workers in Latin America earn as little as 5% of the final price of a banana, for working a 12-13 hour day.

Some plantations fire people who are as young as 25 and replace them with younger people because they cost less and are less likely to know their rights.

Every year one quarter of banana workers in Costa Rica are hospitalized with poisoning from pesticides sprayed on bananas several times a day.

Although Chiquita Brands International made a commitment in November 1998 to seek solutions to problems regarding freedom of association, collective bargaining and protection of workers' health and safety, and to rehabilitate plantations affected by Hurricane Mitch, it has provided no financial assistance other than that required by law.

Working conditions for banana companies typically involve working days of 12-14 hours or more without any overtime payment; wages which are not sufficient to cover the basic needs of subsistence for a family; dismissals without any social security or redundancy payments; lack of medical attention.

In Costa Rica, workers who created a trade union in 1998 have been fired from their jobs, intimidated, and have received death threats. The Costa Rican Rerum Novarum (after the papal encyclical) Workers' Confederation, has had to file a complaint with the International Labor Organization about this problem.

Primary Source: TROCAIRE

Note: For related facts that impact the well being of banana workers, see details of the recent banana trade wars on page 84 .

"We were walking through the plantation when a light shower of rain – or so I thought – began to fall. My local friend pulled me under the shelter of a tree, but my skin had already started to sting and my arms came out in a red rash. The pesticide spray-plane had just flown overhead, as it did several times a day."

Irish Catholic development organization
worker visiting a Chiquita plantation in Honduras

In Indonesia workers for Nike earn $4.76 a day, or a total of $811 (U.S.) a year, many of them earning below the minimum wage.

"We worked from 7:00 a.m. until 6:00 p.m. If they wanted us to work overtime, they would tell us to continue until 9:00. We worked a 14 hour day as often as three times a week. By 1992, I was making US $1.45 a day. On this salary I had to pay $.50 a day for rent and .75 for food. If I missed the factory bus, I would have to use the remaining $.20 for transportation. If you made a mistake on only one pair of shoes, you would be fined $.50."

Cicih Sukaesih, former worker
at a Nike factory in Indonesia

Nike

"You have to meet the quota before you can go home." "She hit all 15 team leaders in turn from the first one to the fifteenth..." "The physical pain didn't last long, but the pain I feel in my heart will never disappear."

Thuy and Lap, woman workers
at Nike plant in Vietnam

"It was very hot, because the machines were so close together. We had to work with glues in those hot conditions. It was very dangerous to our health. We had no gloves and were only given very thin masks. My job was to dip a rubber sole into a chemical, then slap on a cushioned sole. We were expected to produce 2,500 of these soles an hour. If we did not meet our quota, we had to work overtime until we finished. The pace of work was very fast. We were always being pushed to meet production demands."

Facts:
Nike's total revenue for 1997 was $9.19 billion (US), with a profit of $795.8 million. CEO Phil Knight's fourth quarter dividend earnings were $80 million.

In Indonesia workers for Nike earn $4.76 a day, or a total of $811 (US) a year, many of them earning below the minimum wage.

Vietnam's minimum wage is $42 a month. At that rate, labor for a pair of basketball shoes which retail for $149.50 costs Nike $1.50, 1 percent of the retail price.

Workers cannot go to the bathroom more than once per 8-hour shift and they cannot drink water more than twice per shift.

It is a common occurrence for workers to faint from exhaustion, heat, fumes and poor nutrition during their shifts.

.At a factory in Vietnam with 6,000 employees, one doctor works only two hours a day but the factory operates 20 hours a day. Night shift employees do not have any on-site medical emergency services.

Primary sources: Vietnam Labor Watch,
Boycott Nike, National Labor Committee

Wal-Mart

"Going into these factories is like entering prison, where you leave your life outside. The factory owners do not let—and don't want—the young workers to think for themselves. They want them to be stupid. The workers need permission to use the bathroom, and they are told when they can and cannot go. Young women enter these factories at 14, 15, 16 and 17 years old. These young workers entered the maquila with a sixth grade education, with no understanding of the maquila, the companies whose clothing they sew or the forces shaping where they fit into the global economy. They soon feel impotent, seeing that the Ministry of Labor does nothing, or almost nothing, to help defend their rights. Once the women start working in the maquila they often fall into debt. The wages are very low and no one can survive on them."

Jesuit Priest in Honduras

Facts:

All overtime work in Walmart factories in Honduras is obligatory. Failure to work is punished with several days' suspension without pay, or by firing.

Fire exits are blocked. The fire extinguishers are usually empty, and there is no first aid kit.

The factories are often very hot, and given the lack of adequate ventilation in parts of the factories, the air is heavy with lint from the cut clothing. This is especially the case in and near the cutting section. No protective respiratory masks are distributed to the workers.

The bathrooms are filthy, and the workers must ask permission to use them.

All overtime work in Walmart factories in Honduras is obligatory. Failure to work is punished with several days' suspension without pay, or by firing.

It is common for the water to be off two to three hours a day. The stench coming from the bathrooms can be intolerable.

The workers need permission to drink water. If they fail to get permission, they are punished.

The garments the workers are working on are sometimes grabbed by the supervisors and thrown in the workers' faces, while they are screamed at for any "mistake," such as a loose thread hanging out.

No absences are permitted. If a pregnant woman loses a day, or part of it, to go to the health clinic, she is docked two days' wages.

Primary sources: CAFOD,
National Labor Committee, Sweatshop Watch

Strawberries

Since he was 16 years old, Jorge Martinez has picked California strawberries. At the peak of the strawberry season, Martinez arrives in the Central Coast fields as the sun is rising. The sun will be setting when he leaves for home. To pick strawberries requires more than a willingness to end a 12-hour day with red-stained hands and a tired frame. It takes a particular skill and stamina. Strawberries are one of the few crops for which there is no harvesting machinery, nor is there likely to be. Human skill is required.

The fresh strawberry market demands only attractive, red-ripe berries. They are fragile. Martinez will most likely be paid by how many of the berries he picks-more than 10,000 on a good day, for which he will earn less than a penny per berry. Stamina is required, too. Martinez must stoop, his back bent over the foot-high berry plants. To stand and stretch takes him away from the plants and lowers his productivity. The work for most pickers will be done with few amenities. Bathrooms are often dirty. Fresh drinking water is not always present. If Martinez' daughter were to follow in his footsteps, as many farm workers' children do, she may face demands for sex in exchange for employment as some field workers have reported.

As with all farm labor there are other hazards. Martinez suffers from chronic back injuries, yet he has no insurance to pay for medical care. In fact, Martinez fears he will lose his job if he complains about his pain. Each year when the season begins, Martinez and other strawberry workers complain of welts and raised spots on their skin. Several pesticides used by strawberry growers can cause skin rashes and eye irritations. If Martinez is like the average strawberry worker, he'll quit in four years. The strain of the job causes most pickers to give up the work by the time they're 30 years old, worn out.

Facts:
California's 20,000 strawberry workers earn an average of $8,500 a year.

Strawberry workers labor stooped over ankle-high plants for 10 to 12 hours a day in fields treated with pesticides.

Few have adequate health insurance. Workers have to fight to have clean drinking water and bathrooms in the fields.

Many workers return to the same fields year after year, yet they must reapply for the same jobs and can be fired on a whim.

The strawberry industry has revenues of about $650 million a year.

About 80 percent of the nation's fresh strawberries are grown in California.

When workers successfully organized in individual fields in the past, their fields were plowed under in retaliation, leading workers to begin an industry-wide campaign. Firings and harassment continue.

About 80 groups and individuals are supporting a campaign through the National Strawberry Commission for Workers' Rights. The AFL-CIO's more than 600 central labor councils are supporting the workers.

Primary sources: United Farm Workers, the Strawberry Workers Campaign

Georgetown Students Sit-in for Just Labor Practices

In early February, 1999, students at Georgetown University decided that their school's actions to eliminate sweatshop practices were not enough, so they took action themselves. On February fifth, 27 students staged a sit-in in the University President's office, and 85 hours later they emerged, having convinced the University that further, more demanding action must be taken.

These Georgetown students were not engaging in a trivial dispute. Georgetown ranks in the top 20 among universities that produce clothing with their own name or logo, so it plays a large part in the burgeoning industry of sports logo apparel. With close ties to such companies as Gear, Starter, and the Nike corporation, which has fallen under heavy criticism in recent years for tolerating violation of labor rights in its factories, Georgetown is in a position to exert a considerable influence on industry practices. In late November, 1998, a sports apparel conglomerate that includes Georgetown did release a Code of Conduct for companies that hold licenses to produce their clothing. This Code of Conduct addressed some of the violations that had gone unchecked in these factories, but students, after discussing the Code and its ramifications, decided that their university name did not belong on clothing that supports any sweatshop practices.

Citing the Code of Conduct's failure to include a guarantee of a living wage and the disclosure of the location of factories, the Georgetown Solidarity Committee, a student group formed to combat poor labor conditions, rejected the code upon its release and called upon the University Administration to do the same. When it became clear that the university was satisfied with the Code as it stood, the group decided to bring their demands closer to home for the administration. On February 5, the group led 27 students into President Leo J. O'Donovan's office, sat down, and

> Georgetown ranks in the top 20 among universities that produce clothing with their own name or logo, so it plays a large part in the burgeoning industry of sports logo apparel.

would not leave until administrators agreed to their conditions. They had support in their endeavor: the next day, 170 students, from Georgetown and 16 other universities, staged a rally outside the office building in support of the sit-in.

Even though one Georgetown official had said that they had "no interest in signing what we don't believe is achievable," after 85 hours the students convinced the Georgetown administration to try to achieve more anyway. Speaking to a rally of 250 students assembled in front of the President's office building, that same official announced that the University had agreed to require that factory location be disclosed to the University community within a year. This provision is crucial, because as a student organizer put it, "The reason sweatshops exist is because they're hidden. . . If we had full disclosure, the other provisions would fall in line. . . This is the provision that has the [apparel] industry quaking." Missing from the sit-in agreement was the living-wage provision; because of this, the students realize that their work on this issue is not yet over. Their presence will continue to be felt, however: four students, all of whom participated in the sit-in or organized the campaign, will be appointed to the new University committee that will oversee the implementation of labor regulations in factories that produce Georgetown apparel.

Mark Torma

The Spirit of the Lord is upon me and has anointed me . . . to proclaim liberty to captives and to let the oppressed go free.

Luke 4:18

The Jubilee year is made sacred by proclaiming freedom.

Leviticus 25:10

Jubilee freedom liberates us to go home . . . the jubilee even frees us to return to our true selves . . . we are free to be at one with our God, our liberator, our savior and our home.

Preparing for Jubilee, U.S. Catholic Conference

Different forms of slavery

Human beings can be captives and slaves in many ways; certainly the slavery of workers in sweatshops is one of them. So is the sex tourism business in countries such as Asia and Latin America, which keeps vulnerable young girls in impoverished homes, enslaved by brutality and threats. Many other situations keep people in bondage. Some of these include the violent conditions in U.S. jails and prison; violent conditions in disadvantaged neighborhoods; violations of human rights, economic as well as civil and political; the hatred and anger of racists and white supremacists; and addictions to alcohol and drugs, addiction to consuming goods and services and to the fast pace of modern life.

In your groups, discuss the following questions:

Consider this passage by Elizabeth O'Connor: "At the center of our pain, we glimpse a fairer world and hear a call. When we are able to keep company with our own fears and sorrows, we are shown the way to go, our parched lives are watered, and the earth becomes a greener place." Why is it often difficult to recognize our own forms of slavery to feelings, memories, habits, lifestyles? When we recognize some of our own forms of bondage, how can our lives "be watered?"

Can you name some of the kinds of bondage that you may be beginning to see in your own life and in your own local social groups and communities? What are the chains that weigh us down and prevent us from living fully in God's light? Name and discuss some of the specific forms of bondage and enslavement that we can see in communities in the U.S. and in other countries.

Can we be truly free if we ignore the pain and slavery of others? How is our liberation as children of God bound up with the liberation of others? Can you name some individuals who have worked or who are working for the liberation of others? What motivated and sustained them?

How—as a small community—in this discussion group, and in the other groups and communities we are a part of, can we find, and provide, nourishment and support to work toward liberation for ourselves and, in the process, to become liberators working for others?

To: Store manager, _____

From: _____
_____

I and my family and friends would like to continue to buy products from your store, but I want information about the conditions under which the clothes and/or products you sell are made. Your company's head Buyer should be able to provide or locate this information.

Do your company and your suppliers (and all your, and their, contractors and subcontractors who operate factories anyplace in the world, especially in developing countries) all have a code of conduct which is independently monitored? Can you send me a copy of the code and provide information on who monitors the code?

Do your company and your suppliers respect the right of freedom to form unions or other workers' associations?

What steps are your company, and your suppliers' companies, taking to guarantee to consumers that the apparel and products you sell are produced by workers who receive a just and equitable wage, have the right to organize, and work in safe and humane conditions? Will you post this information and your code of conduct in your stores? How else will you inform your customers about the conditions under which your products are made?

I look forward to your reply and to shopping again with you after I receive your response.

Suggestions For Action

1. Find out the ethical standards and labor practices of companies when making apparel and other consumer purchases (see the Interfaith Center on Corporate Responsibility's web site: www.web.net/~robrien/papers/sri/players/iccr.htm)

2. Talk to store managers to find out what policies and procedures companies have to prevent sweatshop abuses in all factories that contribute to the production of a product; hand out or mail sheet #D7 to store managers.

3. Join or start a campaign that works for the end to labor abuses (see resources next page).

4. Write and demand that local, state, and national governments adopt policies and pass laws that protect workers' rights and ensure humane working conditions not only in the U.S. but around the world. (See resources next page)

5. Whenever possible, buy Fair Trade products (visit the Alternative Mall at the Center of Concern's Web site, www.coc.org/coc/).

6. Buy from community-based businesses and support local businesses.

7. Watch and discuss the video, *Global Solidarity: A Framework for Parishes*, from the U.S. Catholic Conference (call 1-800-235-8722) and/or the video, *For Poor and Rich Alike: Understanding Globalization*, by Amata Miller, IHM, from NETWORK Education Program (call 202-547-5556).

As You Sow Foundation/
Corporate Accountability Program
540 Pacific Avenue
San Francisco, CA 94133,
Tel: (415) 391-3212
e-mail: asyousow@igc.org.

Campaign for Labor Rights
1247 E. Street, SE
Washington, DC 20003
Tel: (541) 344-5410
Web site: http://www.compugraph.com/clr

Co-op America
1612 K Street NW, #600
Washington, DC 20006
Tel: (202) 872-5307
Web site: www.coopamerica.org

Council on Economic Priorities
30 Irving Place
New York, NY 10003
Tel: (212) 420-1133.
Web site: http://www-
2.realaudio.com/CEP/home.html

Fair Trade Federation
P.O. Box 126
Barre, MA 01005
Tel: (508) 355-0284.
Web site: www.fairtradefederation.com

Interfaith Center on Corporate Responsibility
475 Riverside Drive, Room 566
New York, NY
Tel: (212) 870-2023
Web site:
http://www.web.net/~robrien/papers/sri/
players/iccr.html

International Labor Rights Fund
733 15th Street NW, Suite 920
Washington, DC 20005
Tel: (202)347-4100
Web site: www.laborrights.org
Investor Responsibility Research Center
350 Connecticut Avenue NW, Suite 700
Washington, DC 20036
Tel: (202) 833-0700
Web site: www.irrc.org

National Consumers League/
Child Labor Coalition
1701 K Street NW, Suite 1200
Washington, DC 20006
Tel: (202) 835-3323
Web site: www.natlconsumersleague.org

National Labor Committee for Worker and
Human Rights (US)
275 Seventh Avenue, 15th Floor
New York, NY 10001
Tel: (212) 242-3002
Web site: http://www.nlcnet.org

Sweatshop Watch
310 8th Street, Suite 309
Oakland, CA 94607
Tel: (510) 834-8990
Web site: www.sweatshopwatch.org

Stop Sweatshops Campaign/UNITE
Union of Needletrades, Industrial and Textile
Employees,
1710 Broadway
New York, NY 10019
Tel: (212) 265-7000
Web site: www.UNITEunion.org

Restore Just Relations

Restore Just Relations

The U.S. cultural concept of justice focuses upon equal opportunity for all, and this is sometimes not understood in the context of justice for all and the common good.

"Restore just relations" is perhaps the most challenging of the biblical Jubilee precepts. It is based on the conviction that all of the resources of creation belong to all of God's people together. When some people accumulate more than they need while others lack basic necessities, there is serious injustice. The biblical vision of Jubilee presumes that this dynamic of accumulation and need will constantly play itself out and therefore requires a periodic redistribution: a fresh start. That helps to eliminate the suffering and animosity that grow between groups when disparities grow too large. It fosters harmony and stability in community life, and the peace of God in our spirits.

The U.S. cultural concept of justice focuses upon equal opportunity for all, and this is sometimes not understood in the context of justice for all and the common good. Redistribution systems are attacked for creating dependency and for taking money away from those in society who have shown that they know how to use it most successfully. Conspicuous wealth, it is argued, provides incentive to people in poverty to work harder and become more competitive. This is a land of opportunity. We must protect equal opportunity for all, we hear; then anyone who really wants to succeed and works hard for it will do well. In this time of globalization, money is to be made everywhere in the world.

The U.S. cultural sense of justice, particularly at this time in our history, has little respect for welfare entitlements or redistribution schemes. Self-responsibility and opportunity dominate the rhetoric. This bootstrap mentality is balanced, though, by our sense of fairness that demands "a level playing field" for everyone. It is not hard to see that when people lack adequate food or health care or education, they do not have "a level playing field." Even though this nation does not yet have a tradition of acknowledging fundamental economic, social and cultural human rights, there is a foundation that can be built upon in our strong commitment to a fair opportunity for both our citizens and for all our brothers and sisters in the global village.

The Church has long called us to go even further, calling for a special option for those in poverty and a special commitment to helping those impoverished at home and around the world. The U.S. Bishops have called on Catholics to make a special Jubilee covenant with those in poverty, and the first activities on the following pages help participants to better understand poverty and to consider drafting their own covenants. The final activity helps participants to recognize the link between growing world poverty and global trade and to reflect on the Church's concern for just global policies.

James E. Hug, S.J.

Restore Just Relations

OPENING PRAYER

Lord you have given us a world full of rich resources to feed us all, and to provide us with all that body and mind could need, yet the poor are still with us—deprived of food, of homes, of education, of dignity, deprived of healing and hope.
Lord Have Mercy.

For all our confessions of faith that have not led us to the needs of our brothers and sisters,
For all protestations of love for You that have not included love for all your children,
For all our chasing after selfish dreams and striving after success, Forgive us.
Christ Have Mercy.

Forgive our unwillingness to share, forgive our politics and commerce that exclude rather than include all children of God.
Forgive us for leaving Christ hungry, homeless, neglected and abandoned.
Forgive us so we can bring ourselves back to you and to your human family.
Lord Have Mercy.

REFLECTIONS

The riches of creation were to be considered as a common good. The Jubilee year was meant to restore this social justice.

Pope John Paul II,
On the Coming of the Third Millennium

The proposal of a new style of life applies to all Christians living in America. This conversion demands a genuine identification with the personal style of Jesus Christ, who leads us to simplicity, poverty, and responsibility for others and the renunciation of our own advantage.

Pope John Paul II, *The Church in America*

Jubilee is an all-encompassing vision of social and ecological justice that calls for release from bondage, redistribution of wealth, and renewal of earth. This celebration of Jubilee is meant to restore equality among all the children of Israel, offering new possibilities to families that had lost their property and even their personal freedom. The riches of creation were to be considered a common good of the whole of humanity. The Jubilee year was meant to restore this social justice.

Canadian Ecumenical Jubilee Initiative

CLOSING PRAYER

We cannot merely pray to you, O God, to end starvation; for you have already given us the resources with which to feed the entire world—if we can use them wisely.

We cannot merely pray to you, O God, to root out injustice; for you have already given us the power to stand up against wrong and to live in solidarity with the poor—if we could only commit to this power for good.

Therefore we pray to you instead, O God, for strength, determination and willpower, to do instead of just pray—to become truly your daughters and sons, to share the results of our labor, the possessions and resources we were given, and to be builders of your Kingdom, bringing hope and justice to the poor.

ACTIVITY 1:
CREATING A COVENANT WITH THE POOR

"By making a covenant with the poor we are making God's covenant and special concern for the poor our own." (*Why Should Your School make a New Covenant with the Poor?*, CAFOD)

The U.S. Bishops have suggested that parishes, schools, small faith communities and/or families make a Covenant with the people in poverty to appropriately observe Jubilee and to join in the work to restore justice in the new millennium. This activity will provide information on poverty and the Church's Option for the Poor, and it will offer a model covenant that can be adapted in any way to fit the needs of your group/class.

1. Divide the group into small groups if you have more than eight participants. Appoint a facilitator for each group. Ask all group participants to go to sheet #E1, which is a process for contemplating what it really means to be poor.

Note: The exercise on becoming a poverty statistic focuses on what it is like to be poor in developing countries. You may choose to re-write it to focus on those living in poverty in the U.S.; unfortunately, not many changes would have to be made in the living conditions.

2. After giving time for each participant to read, think and write, have the group share their stories as "poverty statistics." After the discussion, ask all the participants if any of their ideas about the poor changed as a result of this exercise. How do their peers usually define "poor" and what misconceptions about the poor have they heard?

3. Ask all participants to read sheet #E2, which gives some background on poverty. Given the statistics on poverty, and the Church's call for us to be especially concerned about the poor, challenge each group to draw up a model Covenant with the Poor, using sheet #E3 for suggestions. Have groups share at the end of a 15-20 minute discussion period.

You may choose instead to have all the participants suggest activities that will go into a Covenant and write these on a board or flip chart so they can be discussed by the entire group.

4. Plan a Commitment Ceremony. At such a ceremony, the group can read their Covenant with the Poor out loud together after a time of prayer and reflection. Then ask each participant to go to where the Covenant is posted and write her/his name on that document as a sign of her/his commitment and involvement in the fulfillment of the covenant. End with a period of silence and a prayer of hope.

AND

ACTIVITY 2:
POVERTY: WHAT'S TRADE GOT TO DO WITH IT?

Divide into small groups. Copy and distribute sheets #E4, #E5, and #E6 which have information on justice and trade, and case studies about unjust trade policies. Have the participants read #E4 for background, then discuss the questions on #E5 and #E6 after reviewing the case studies. Have a wrap-up discussion on how this information challenges us to become more informed about what is happening in the new global society and how it affects all our brothers and sisters in Christ.

Living in Poverty

Poverty is:

- . to experience not having the basic necessities of shelter, food, health care, education for a family or for oneself; it is to experience that survival is a struggle.
- . to experience what it means to be insignificant or undesirable for whatever reason: gender, sexual identity, class, race, past history or reputation.
- . to experience being pushed away or excluded from the ordinary exchanges of society because of physical or mental disease or handicap that others find frightening or disturbing in any way.
- . to experience being a faceless person, someone without a name, someone whose reality is invisible to the majority of people, someone whose life does not matter to the whole and perhaps not even to any part of the whole.
- . to experience being a burden to others.
- . to come to believe that not only is this the way things are, but that this is the way things are supposed to be - for me, for us. The final indignity of poverty is that it robs people of hope in the possibility of a better way of being.

Estelle Demers, "Our One World Reality: Poverty and Wealth"

Becoming a "Poverty Statistic"

To imagine that you are a poor person, a "poverty statistic," go through the following process.

Imagine how a typical United States family, living in a small suburban house, could be transformed into an equally typical family of the underdeveloped world.

First, in your imagination, strip the house of its furniture. Everything goes: beds, chairs, tables, television sets, lamps. Leave the family with a few old blankets, a kitchen table, a wooden chair. Each member of the family may keep his/her oldest suit or dress, a shirt or blouse. A pair of shoes goes to the head of the family, but none for the wife and children. In the kitchen, turn to the cabinets. A box of matches may stay, a small bag of flour, some sugar and salt. A few moldy potatoes already in the garbage must be hastily rescued, for they will provide much of tonight's meal. Leave a handful of onions, a dish of dried beans. Take away all the rest: the meat, the fresh vegetables, the canned goods, the crackers, the candy.

Strip the house of all amenities: the bathroom is dismantled, the running water shut off, the electric wires taken out. Next, take away the house. The family moves to the tool shed.

Communications must go next. No more newspapers, magazines, books—not that they are missed, since the family's literacy goes, as well.

Now government services must go. No more postman, no more fireman. There is a school, but it is three miles away and consists of two classrooms. They are not too overcrowded since only a few children in the neighborhood go to school and the school costs money. There are, of course, no hospitals or doctors nearby. The nearest clinic is ten miles away and is tended by a midwife. It can be reached by bicycle, but it is a very difficult ride. Or one can go by bus—not always inside, but there is usually room on top.

Finally, money. The family can have five dollars. Meanwhile, the head of the family must earn his keep. As a peasant cultivator with three acres to tend, he may raise the equivalent of $100 to $300 worth of crops a year. If he is a tenant farmer, which is more than likely, a third or so of his crop will go to his landlord and probably another ten percent to the local money lender.

And so our typical United States family is down to the very bottom of the human scale. It is, however, a bottom in which we can find, give or take a hundred million souls, at least a billion people.

Adapted from Robert Heilbroner,
The Ascent (New York: Harper, 1963).

After the exercise, pick a specific identity as a person in poverty. For example, you may be a mother of five children living in Africa, or one of the children. Think of an autobiographical story that goes with your identity. Consider who you are, where you live, the reason that you are poor and how has being poor affected you. Are you male or female, young or old? Do you live in the U.S. or in another country? Write down a little about yourself, how you see yourself and how you feel about yourself.

Reflection on Poverty and the Poor

Overcoming poverty has become the most urgent issue facing all countries and societies today. Around the world more than two billion people have little or no access to food, basic services or adequate shelter, and 12 million children die each year of curable diseases or malnutrition before their fifth birthday. Nine hundred million people globally are either unemployed or under-employed.

United Nations Non-Governmental Liaison Service,
Go Between 72, Dec. 98-Jan. 99

In 1996, approximately 36.5 million people in the United States (13.7%) had income that fell beneath the official U.S. Poverty Line of $16,450 per year. In 1992, 12% of Whites, 33% of African Americans and 29% of Latinos lived below the poverty line. In 1992, 22% of our children (a decline of 5% since 1959) and 13% of people older than 65 (a decline of 22% since 1959) were in poverty.

Poverty and Faith Justice,
Catholic Campaign for Human Development

The poor of the United States and of the world are your sisters and brothers in Christ. You must never be content to leave them just the crumbs from the feast. You must take of your substance, and not just of your abundance, in order to help them. And you must treat them like guests at your family table. . . The parable of the rich man and Lazarus must always be present in our memory; it must form our conscience. Christ demands openness to our brothers and sisters in need — openness from the rich, the affluent, the economically advanced; openness to the poor, the under-developed and the disadvantaged. Christ demands an openness that is more than benign attention, more than token actions or half-hearted efforts that leave the poor as destitute as before or even more. . . Riches and freedom create a special obligation.

Pope John Paul II,
Address at Yankee Stadium, New York, 1979

It is well known how strong were the words used by the Fathers of the Church to describe the proper attitude of persons who possess anything towards persons in need. To quote Saint Ambrose: 'You are not making a gift of your possessions to the poor persons. You are handing over to them what is theirs. For what has been given in common for the use of all, you have arrogated to yourself. The world is given to all, and not only to the rich.' That is, private property does not constitute for anyone an absolute and unconditioned right. No one is justified in keeping for exclusive use what is not needed, when others lack necessities.

Pope Paul VI, *Encyclical Letter
on the Development of Peoples,* 1967

Feminization of poverty is a new term for a very old problem. Historically and presently, those most affected by poverty and least able to escape it have been, and continue to be, women.

The Feminization of Poverty: Background Paper,
Catholic Charities USA, 1986

To build a community of justice means making changes in personal lifestyles that reduce the waste of environmental and natural resources, thus enabling others to have a sufficient share of the goods of God's creation. The task is personal, enormous and global. We Christians are blessed with critical optimism - the virtue of hope, believing a better future is possible but knowing it is not inevitable. In our hope, we know it is not necessary that what we do solves the problem, but that what we do has meaning.

Preferential Option for the Poor,
Book IV, Campaign for Human Development

Sample Options for your Covenant with the Poor

A covenant with the poor is a way of working to make our vision of a better world a reality. It is a practical way of focusing our concern on what kind of world we want future generations to inherit. Whatever else we do for the millennium, we need to work to ensure that the world is a better place for everyone, especially those suffering in poverty. (*Why Should Your School make a New Covenant with the Poor?* CAFOD)

You may choose any or all of the options below, you may reword them to match your situation, and/or you may include other ideas and activities in your own covenant. Try to be generous and challenge yourself to take seriously your Catholic faith's option for the poor.

1. Wealth Sharing
We promise:
- to use our education and skills to help others improve their lives by assisting people to learn to read, and/or to develop language skills, computer literacy, to learn job skills, with job training and placement, etc.
- to give our time to be present to the sick, the housebound, the elderly, asylum seekers/refugees, and others who are marginalized in our communities and to act as their advocates, giving a voice to the voiceless.

- to encourage acts of "underconsumption" each Friday of the year, buying and eating less food and other products and donating saved money to economic development projects, both locally and globally, through groups like Catholic Relief Services.
  - to see Lent and Advent as times to make sacrifices that will benefit those in poverty in some way.
  - to be more moderate and less wasteful in our use and consumption of basic utilities and water.
  - to make a contribution for a hungry child every time we purchase a non-essential food item (keep an envelope in your purse, or a box in your car, and regularly send the contents to Catholic Relief Services or a local agency that feeds the hungry).
  - to commit to work in our parish to set aside, for the poor at home and overseas, a percentage of all funds raised for parish building or refurbishment projects.
  - to donate 10% of funds raised at bazaars, church fairs, etc., to those in poverty at home and overseas.
  - to contribute to a scholarship fund (or set up such a fund) to provide a child from a low-income family with a good education at a local school and to provide tutoring and mentoring for the child, and for other children who need support.
  - Other _____

2. Social Justice Activities

We promise:

- to encourage parishioners/school community members to buy fairly traded goods and to use fairly traded tea and coffee at parish and school events.
- to become involved and support the work of the diocesan/parish/school social justice group(s).
- to actively seek information on issues such as welfare reform from the U.S. Catholic Conference and the local diocesan peace and justice office
- to support local diocese and ecumenical initiatives aimed at tackling domestic poverty issues such as unemployment and homelessness.
- to invite speakers from local agencies working with the poor and from organizations that are working on poverty in other parts of the world (such as the Maryknoll Missionaries) to give talks to the parish/school community to increase understanding of poverty-related issues at special times during the year.
- to start a monthly study group to read and discuss articles related to world poverty, trade, and international debt (materials from the Center of Concern and United States Catholic Conference are useful for this).
- to write to our local and national leaders as a group to support policies, legislation and programs to overcome poverty (NETWORK, the National Catholic Lobby group, has a monthly newsletter that gives more details on poverty legislation).
- to write to the federal government to re-allocate tax dollars to provide basic services for those children living in poverty.
- To engage in policy advocacy on a range of social justice issues
- Other _____

3. Prayer and Liturgy

We promise:

- to be present to the pain and the needs of those in poverty in a daily prayer time.
- to include in the prayers at each Mass in our parish and/or school prayers for policies and actions that will end poverty in the new millennium.
- to use the offertory procession in our parish as a focus for our gifts to the poor and an occasion to celebrate what we receive from those in poverty.
- to encourage our musicians to use hymns that reflect a concern for justice.
- to include a focus on the needs of the poor in our children's liturgies.
- to start a prayer group that keeps informed on local and international poverty-related problems and regularly prays for specific needs of those in poverty in these situations.
- to include a justice dimension to our parish/school's catechetical/sacrament preparation programs.
- to include a justice dimension in confirmation training at our parish/school.
- to review, rewrite and renew our covenant with the poor each year on a special day.
- Other _____

Poverty: What's Trade Got to Do with it?

1. How is trade defined in our global economy?

Whenever we talk about international trade, there are always at least two countries involved, since trade is an exchange of goods and services. For example, a company in one country will sell garments that it makes to earn money to buy the airplanes of another country. The exporting country would have to make many garments in order to import one airplane.

2. Why should Catholics be interested in international trade?

Trade and investment are becoming increasingly important issues in the work for global economic justice and our church's Option for the Poor. Growing global and regional economic integration and "free trade" have been widening the gap between those with wealth and those who live in poverty, both between countries and within countries. Advocates of the current direction of global economic liberalization speak glibly of "winners and losers" but offer little to mitigate the poverty of the so-called losers. Catholic Social Teaching demands that trade and investment policies promote the full realization of human rights, the rights of workers over the right to profit, the responsibility of the state to guarantee citizens' full participation and well-being, the promotion of justice among all nations and care for the earth's limited resources. The challenges before all people of faith and good will is to shape trade and investment systems that increase equity among nations and peoples. The goal is both sustainable development within the limitation of the earth's environment, sustainable livelihoods for all women, men, families, and communities, and equitable sharing of the world's resources.

3 Who has the "upper hand" in trade?

Products made by developed countries are capital-intensive, meaning they depend on the heavy use of physical capital in the form of machinery and equipment as well as financial capital in the form of stocks, bonds, derivatives, and the like. Any processing done by developing countries relies on their relatively lower skilled labor, producing labor-intensive commodities. Thus, trade between developed countries and developing countries means the developed countries sell high-end products for low-end commodities of the developing, poorer countries. This arrangement perpetuates the unequal distribution of assets and the resources of Creation. Economic assets and political power at the global level are concentrated on a few countries (and in elite groups within those countries), such as the United States, Germany, and Japan. Through trade, these countries are able to further increase their assets while developing countries are stuck in their stage of development.

4. Who is receiving favored status in trade negotiations?

Multinational corporations and banks have an increasing amount of influence not only in policy making but also, and more importantly, in terms of manipulating the prices of currencies and commodities, the levels of production, and consumer demand. As the main producers of various goods and services, the multinational corporations are able to set the prices according to their desired profit levels. In the same manner, they can control the amount of goods and services being produced, making them scarce or abundant as they please. Large spending on marketing and advertising heavily influences demand for their products. Because of the influential presence of multinational corporations, it is not surprising to find that official government policy is in their favor so that international trade agreements reflect their concerns and protect their interests. At negotiating tables such as the World Trade Organization, developing countries (many of whom were former colonies of the developed countries) are unable to gain a fairer trading environment since they come from a weakened position. Thus millions of poor people in these developing countries have no real voice at the bargaining tables of world power.

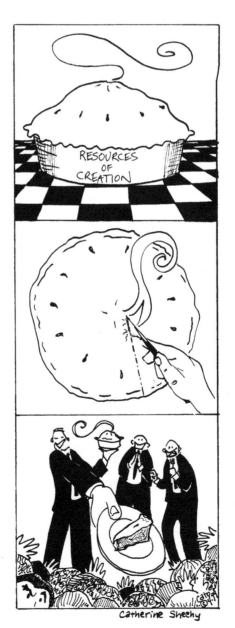

Catherine Sheehy

5. What is the result of recent trade negotiations?

Unequal exchange is maintained by a set of trade policy instruments that favor the strong. Tariffs—taxes on imported commodities—and quotas—limitations on quantities that can be imported—are frequently implemented for developing country exports, while the developing countries are forced to lower their tariffs and remove their quotas to open their economies to trade from the richer countries.

Meanwhile, workers in developed countries are pitted against workers in developing countries. The loss of jobs in developed countries, such as the U.S., is blamed on the low wages of developing countries. The reality is that the profit motive of multinational corporations signifies their willingness to eliminate jobs in their home countries in order to hire people in developing countries at substandard wage rates and not provide just working conditions.

6. What does a commitment to Justice call us to do regarding trade issues?

Trade policies will increasingly determine the quality of life for everyone in the global village. Small, poor economies cannot compete with larger, wealthier economies or transnational corporations on an equal footing. We must advocate fair accommodations for these countries to ensure the ability of local enterprises to generate local wealth on a sustainable basis, or poverty will continue despite other development efforts and charitable donations from our communities.

See the resource section to see how you can connect with efforts to promote fair trade and thus to restore a more equal sharing of creation's resources.

"**Under free trade the strong compete with the weak, the developed with the underdeveloped. International cooperation and regulation are needed to protect weak and vulnerable countries in the transition to full participation in the global economy.**"

(*The Common Good*, Statement of the
Catholic Bishops of England and Wales, 1998)

Trade Case Studies

1). Read the news article below and discuss the problems of the Bolivian Indians in the context of the U.S. Bishops' statement on Developing Nations (below). If you were representing the Bishops at a meeting with U.S. delegates the World Trade Organization (an organization that is similar to the United Nations and decides on international trade policies through delegates from various countries), what would you propose they negotiate regarding the situation in Bolivia, and why?

Case Study #1

INDIGENOUS PEOPLE IN DEVELOPING COUNTRIES LOSING JOBS AND BENEFITS

By Stella Danker

UNITED NATIONS – Despite the international trend toward open markets, groups looking after the interests of indigenous peoples say that free trade has been bad for the environment and native people. They say they want an independent study done on the impact of open markets on their communities at a time when the World Trade Organization (WTO) is "forcing" more developing countries toward globalization.

Aurora Donoso of Ecuador, representing Accion Ecologica, said: "There is a lot of pressure from corporations to factor laws for their investment as a national priority. For example in mining, corporations have priority over the water more than the local people in agriculture."

Carol Kalafatic, a Bolivian Indian who is the New York representative for the International Indian Treaty Council, said: "Tens of thousands of people are being laid off because of privatization. There are even more strikes now, and lots of protests in both the capital and smaller cities outside. People are out of work."

She said that foreign investors buying up her country's assets represented "the selling off of Bolivia."

Indigenous peoples, who are already at the bottom rung of society, suffer the most. They shared their views in a discussion titled "The Proposed WTO Millennium Round – Against Sustainable Development?" organized by the Third World Network (TWN) and the Tektebba Foundation, which looks after the interests of indigenous peoples in the Philippines. Charles Arden-Clarke, head of the World Wide Fund for Nature's Trade and Investment Unit, called for governments and other experts to provide relevant case studies on the impact, both positive and negative, of trade liberalization.

He said they should do this to prepare for the next round of trade negotiations in January 2000. "We can't trust the World Trade Organization to monitor itself," he said. "There is inertia in the UN system."

Quick to share her country's experience was Anita Pleumarom, who coordinates TWN's Tourism and Monitoring Team in Bangkok. "Until two years ago, everybody was into the globalization drive; nobody questioned it," she said, but added that it had turned out to be a disaster for Thailand.

To qualify for an International Monetary fund bailout when the Thai economy went into free fall, the government had to amend several laws, further opening its markets, she said. "There's a new foreign business law which allows for a foreign business to take over a local business 100 percent.

With the debt restructuring, foreign investors can buy Thai assets cheaply. And the strict land laws of the country are also opening up. People in the street are calling this a national sellout," she said.

From the U.S. Catholic Bishops' pastoral letter on the U.S. Economy, Economic Justice for All

Traditional Catholic teaching on global interdependence emphasizes the dignity of the human person, the unity of the human family, the universally beneficial purpose of the goods on the earth as well as the good of each nation. The U.S. plays a leading role in the international economic system, and we are concerned that the U.S. relations with all nations reflect this teaching and be marked by fairness and mutual respect.

The demands of CHRISTIAN LOVE and HUMAN SOLIDARITY challenge all economic actors to choose community over chaos and recognize the moral bonds among all people. BASIC JUSTICE implies that all peoples are entitled to participate in the increasingly interdependent global economy in a way that ensures their freedom and dignity. We want a world that works fairly for all. RESPECT FOR HUMAN RIGHTS, both political and economic, implies that international decisions, institutions and policies must be shaped by values that are more than economic. The creation of a global order in which these rights are secure for all must be a prime objective for all relevant actors on the international stage. THE SPECIAL PLACE FOR THE POOR in this moral perspective means that meeting the basic needs of the millions of deprived and hungry people must be the number one objective of all international policy.

These perspectives constitute a call for fundamental reform in the international economic order. Catholic teaching emphasizes not only the individual conscience, but also the political, legal and economic structures through which policy is determined and issues are adjudicated.

2). Read Case Studies #2 & 3. Discuss how the trade policies in both case studies can have an impact on families in South Africa (case study #2) and Latin America (case study #3). How is the right to profit dominating other rights—to work, to food and basic necessities—in these cases? Why do so many people believe the right to profit is more important than other rights? What would be a just resolution based on the Church's teachings?

Case Study #2

EUROPE IS DESTROYING SOUTH AFRICA'S CANNED FRUIT TRADE

By Action Network, Comhlamh, Cork, Ireland

"I stopped working on November 14th. Christmas was looking at us, then Easter… No more R500 a week. I took home R500 a week. And the children don't understand… And now I am under the hospital for high blood pressure, stress, depression. You lie in bed and look at the ceiling, and in the morning you are still looking at the ceiling. When you are working nothing worries you" –

Salina Kruger, unemployed canning worker

In October 1997, because of the distorted position of South African canned fruit on the EU market, Langeberg Food Processors closed one of their two plants, the Paarl plant, with the loss of 400 permanent jobs and between 3,000 and 4,000 seasonal jobs (most of them for women who depended on Langeberg for years). The factory was, until then, Paarl's main employer. There were knock-on effects too: the Paarl based food canning plant which supplied packaging materials to Langeberg lost jobs, as did local farms. All in all, it is estimated that 800 further farm jobs and perhaps 4,000 seasonal jobs remain under threat.

"Help save our jobs!" demand South African workers. Just last year, European trade policies destroyed more than 2,500 jobs in South African fruit and vegetable canning alone, with another 4,500 under threat. One former worker, Mary April, summed it up. "There is no bright future; because of this poverty we don't have clothes to buy for our children and we don't know what they are going to eat for their supper."

The canning industry is of crucial importance to the people of South Africa's Western Cape. It employs more than 15,000 directly, and over 36,000 indirectly. It is an industry that could be helping South Africa rebuild after apartheid. By imposing huge tariffs on South African fruit, Europe is blocking their exports from European markets. No wonder last year two significant fruit canneries in the Western Cape had to abandon production!

The impact of this unfair support isn't hard to predict: already, South African growers and canners of tomatoes have found it hard to sell their produce even in their home market! 7,500 jobs depend on tomato canning alone, but European producers have flooded the market at well below the costs of domestic production.

That's the impact in Africa; then there are the import duties into Europe. Any South African producer trying to sell their canned fruit in Ireland faces duties of between 10% and 23%. South Africa used to compensate its own farmers for the discrimination; but in 1997, in order to comply with World Trade Organization rules, this compensation was phased out.

As Ghana's Ambassador to the UN, Kofi Awoonor, said, *"while they are telling us that in Africa you cannot subsidize the farmer, there is no country in the western world that does not subsidize agriculture."*

Case Study #3

LATIN AMERICA SLIPS ON THE BANANA TRADE ISSUE

By C. Gerald Fraser

As the saying goes, "When two elephants fight it's the grass that suffers." An illustration of this is the U.S.-European Union (EU) banana trade fracas. Whenever the issues are settled, in all likelihood the farmers and laborers in the small island developing states of the Caribbean will be "grass".

Devoid of the intricacies of foreign trade, the banana issue boils down to corporate greed. Thirty-eight percent of the bananas imported into Europe come from the Caribbean. Almost two-thirds, 62 percent, of the bananas consumed in Europe are Latin American bananas. For the three U.S.-based corporations that dominate the worldwide trade in bananas, Chiquita, Dole, and Del Monte, these percentages are not enough.

The European Union gave importing preference to bananas produced in former European – mainly French and British – colonies in the Caribbean. The EU argues that Caribbean territories have several disadvantages. These include poor soil, sometimes hostile weather, and less than satisfactory growing terrain. More significantly, the EU says, Caribbean farmers usually run small, independent operations. They can't benefit from economies of scale. They can't match the vertically-integrated setups that result in, among other things, lower shipping costs for the big transnationals. Bananas in Europe cost more than they do in the U.S. because the Europeans believe it is just to give preference to these small farmers who have to charge more (larger plantations can be run on a cheaper bottom line).

The U.S., fronting for Dole, Del Monte, and the biggest banana of them all, Chiquita, went to the World Trade Organization to complain that the EU was discriminating. These three corporations own banana plantations in Central and South America. Their historic management of these plantations has turned countries such as Honduras, Guatemala, Costa Rica, and Nicaragua into "banana republics" and enabled the corporations to play inordinate roles in each nation's governance.

The WTO ruled recently that EU preference for Caribbean bananas was illegal. The U.S. is therefore entitled, the WTO says, to collect millions of dollars, in sanctions, from EU countries to pay back the U.S. for trade losses.

Farmers and politicians in the Caribbean are in shock. In Dominica, 20,000 of the 35,000 people employed work in the banana industry. Jamaica now has about 1,800 small farms, averaging five acres each, growing bananas. In 1997 there were 4,000. The president of the All Island Growers Association, Bobby Pottinger, says the WTO places the Caribbean banana industry "in an uncertain position." Some Caribbean diplomats in the corridors of the United Nations have asked, "What do they want us to do? Get into the drug trade to feed our people?"

Suggestions For Action

1. Do more research on poverty in the U.S. and the world, and share what you learn in various ways.

2. Learn more about the Church's Option for the Poor through books and information on the United States Catholic Conference's web site and the Vatican's web site.

3. Seek groups working with poor people at home and abroad to see how you can become involved with their work for justice.

Resources

Alliance for Responsible Trade
927 15th Street, NW, 4th Floor
Washington, DC 20005
Tel: (202) 898-1566
Fax: (202) 898-1612

Center of Concern
1225 Otis Street NE
Washington, DC 20017
Phone: (202) 635-2757
Fax: (202) 832-9494
Web site: www.coc.org/coc/
e-mail: coc@coc.org

The Holy See (Vatican)
Web site: http://www.vatican.va/

United for a Fair Economy
37 Temple Place 5th floor
Boston, MA 02111
Tel: (617) 423-2148
Fax: (617) 423-0191
e-mail: stw@stw.org

United States Catholic Conference
Office of Social Development/World Peace
3211 Fourth Street NE
Washington, DC 200171194.
Tel: (202) 541-3000
Fax: (202) 541-3322
Web site: www.nccbuscc.org

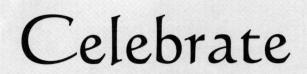

Celebrate

SECTION 6

Celebrate

Celebrate? How can we celebrate when there is so much to repent? The psalmist in exile complained: For there our captors demanded of us songs, And our tormentors mirth, saying, "Sing us one of the songs of Zion." How can I sing the songs of Zion in a foreign land?

[Ps. 137:3]

AN UNUSUAL DISCIPLINE

Jubilee preparations emphasize five themes: *Let the land lie Fallow. Forgive Debts. Free Prisoners and Slaves. Establish Justice. Celebrate.*

How can we celebrate when the land and its people are being trashed and worked to death? How can we celebrate when debt burdens crush more than a billion of our most vulnerable sisters and brothers on the planet? How can we celebrate when so many women, children, families and communities are enslaved in poverty, their most fundamental human rights violated? How can we celebrate when the gap between wealthy and poor is growing so rapidly with such vicious impact?

On the other hand, if we can't celebrate, how can we keep hope alive? If we can't celebrate, how can we believe? If we can't celebrate, how can we have the courage to look honestly at the road ahead or inspire others to join us in the journey?

In the last sermon before his martyrdom, Martin Luther King Jr. imagined himself with God looking at the whole panorama of human history. God asked him what age he would like to live in, and he surveyed them all: biblical times, the classical periods, Renaissance and Reformation, the civil war, the industrial revolution, the depression and the New Deal. . . He finally asked God for the privilege of living a few years in the sickness, injustice, trouble and confusion of the second half of the twentieth century.

"I know, somehow, that only when it is dark enough, can you see the stars. And I see God working in this period of the twentieth century in a way that [people], in some strange way, are responding — something is happening in our world. The masses of people are rising up. And wherever they are assembled today, whether they are in Johannesburg, South Africa; Nairobi, Kenya; Accra, Ghana; New York City; Atlanta, Georgia; Jackson, Mississippi; or Memphis, Tennessee—the cry is always the same — We want to be free."

(from "I See the Promised Land"
in *A Testament of Hope: The Essential Writings
and Speeches of Martin Luther King, Jr.*)

If we can't celebrate, it may well be because we are not paying attention to God working in this period of the twentieth century in the ways people are rising up. The African American Christian community — still fighting its way out of the discrimination and disadvantage left from centuries of slavery — has given us a song from its darkest nights to sing while still in exile:

We've come a long way. We've come a long way.
Sometimes it was an uphill journey
Sometimes on the rough side of the mountain
But we've come a long way. We've come a long way.
Leaning and depending on Jesus, we've come a long way.

In the twentieth century, we have come to risk the very survival of our planet and our people with the driven-ness of our production and consumption patterns. But also in this century, we have begun to see the effects of our actions and calculate our environmental impacts and limits. Young people are standing up to speak out against abuses. People are questioning the value of consuming more and more. There are stars to see; God is working. *We've come a long way.*

In the twentieth century we have watched the burden of crushing debt fall upon innocent families and communities; we continue to witness inhumane trade and finance policies snatching away the hard-earned livelihoods and health of the most vulnerable families and communities in the global economy—dashing their dreams. But we are also seeing millions of people around the world standing together to demand Jubilee relief for the poorest debtor countries and peoples, and we see the leaders of the world's seven most powerful nations responding. It remains an uphill journey before all the burdens can be lifted. But we're not alone on the journey, and *we've come a long way.*

In the twentieth century we continue to encounter multiple forms of discrimination in every society, massive systematic attempts at genocide, the enslavement of the poor in sweat-shops and prisons, horrific war crimes against women, children, men, the elderly. But also in this century we have seen the dismantling of the legal superstructures of slavery and the formal end of the era of empires. The numbers of free nations and peoples in the world have more than doubled. We have become much more aware of the many dimensions of discrimination among us, as peoples around the earth have stood up to call for liberation and freedom. The human rights of every individual, of communities and of the earth itself have been proclaimed and enshrined in international law as the standards to which nations call each other. There are still long, difficult paths ahead, but *we've come a long way*.

In the twentieth century, we have watched the poorest people get poorer and more desperate while the wealthiest people continue to increase their control over the gifts of God's creation intended to meet the needs of all peoples. The wealthiest 3 people in the world have more riches than the 48 poorest countries. We spend more on cosmetics in the U.S. each year than it would take to provide basic education to everyone in the world that lacks it; we spend more on pet food in the U.S. and Europe than it would take to provide adequate nutrition and basic health care to the more than one billion people on the planet without it. (United Nations Development Programme [UNDP] **Human Development Report 1998**) And yet in this century, we have also become aware for the first time of these stunning injustices, and now we can assess our priorities more perceptively and realistically. In this century, we have reduced poverty more than in the previous five centuries. We have come to the point where we can see that "eradicating severe poverty in the first decades of the 21st century is feasible." (UNDP **Human Development Report 1997**) There are certainly many political hurdles on the journey ahead. But God is at work. And *we've come a long way*.

When I speak or write of the challenges facing us as we work for Jubilee at this time in history, people too often complain of feeling overwhelmed and paralyzed. I have often responded that if we keep our eyes on those suffering most under the injustices of our systems, we will realize **we cannot afford the luxury of paralysis**.

It will perhaps be more empowering to point out that when we look at how far we've come during the last century, when we contemplate in that journey the crystallized dreams, creativity, dedication and sacrifice of millions upon millions of people just like us, we can realize that our challenges and efforts are just the current edge of the powerful, untiring press of the Spirit. "It is right for us to give You thanks and praise: all life, all holiness—all efforts to renew the land and its peoples, to forgive debts, to free prisoners and slaves, to establish justice—come from You through the working of the Holy Spirit. Let your Spirit come upon us and our gifts to make them holy so that they may become for us the body and blood of Jesus, the Christ." [Adaptation of Eucharistic Prayer III]

Go, and celebrate the Spirit!

James E. Hug, S.J.

OPENING PRAYER

O God our creator and sustainer, we pray to you:
We want to celebrate life.
We cry out against all that kills life:
    hunger, poverty, unemployment, sickness, debt,
    repression, individualism, abuse of the earth,
    injustice, and all other forms of slavery.
We want to announce fullness of life:
    work, education, health, housing,
    safe environment, bread for all.
We want communion, solidarity, a world renewed.
We hope against hope.
With the God of history,
We want to make things new again.

REFLECTIONS

This Jubilee theme was central to Jesus' understanding of how things should be. This characterizes all the activity of Jesus. Pope John Paul II also sees this millennium celebration as a teaching moment for the Church, a universal call to action that all may share in the fullness of life.

Ed O'Connell, *The Millennium Jubilee*

What do we see in Christ's life of the Jubilee spirit? How can you keep the Spirit of Jubilee alive in yourself and how can you celebrate the hope that Jubilee signifies in your own heart? In your community? In your school/parish?

Celebrate

CLOSING PRAYER

O God of great compassion,
You called us to serve the cause of justice
And to be messengers of Your love
To those the world has forgotten.
As we go forth in the knowledge
That you are with us always,
Help us to use our energy, our love and power
To transform Your earth through prayer and action.
Bless each of us in the days ahead.
Bless our efforts to serve the poor and the
disadvantaged.
Bless our hopes to work for the fullness of life, for
peace and dignity for all
Bless our celebrations and fill us with Your joy.
We make this prayer through Christ our Lord.
Amen.

Activities

ACTIVITY 1: A MILLENNIUM CELEBRATION

A. Divide into small groups. Ask each group to design a prayerful celebration for the beginning of the new millennium. To begin, have the participants read over the opening essay by Fr. Hug, the Prayer Service on sheet #F1 and the Eucharist Celebration on sheet #F2. They may adapt one of these services, use parts of both, or design a different kind of service. Have the all the groups report on what they think would make a meaningful service for themselves. Encourage setting actual times to hold the service(s).

AND/OR

ACTIVITY 2: CREATING A JUBILEE BANNER

Note: You can have your participants do the planning and construction of a banner or wall hanging in one session, or have them do the planning in one session (they should have a sketched-out design) and the actual construction at another time. Materials, such as felt, burlap, etc. and cloth scraps, magic markers, fabric glue, etc. will be necessary.

1. Divide into small groups. Have the participants read the opening essay by Fr. Hug and the reflection and the directions on sheet #F3.
2. Brainstorm on how these reflections and other aspects of Jubilee justice can be embodied in images, signs, pictures, etc. Work out a design that captures at least some of these.
3. Have participants share their final designs. Discuss how these banners can be used in the Jubilee year ahead to celebrate and to promote hope for social justice throughout the world.

AND/OR

ACTIVITY 3: CELEBRATE SIGNS OF HOPE IN DEVELOPING COUNTRIES

With your entire group or in small groups, plan a series of celebratory sessions, to be held in the Jubilee Year, on countries from the developing world. Use sheet #F4 to design the series.

A Prayer Service on the Threshold of the New Millennium

A. Prepare a place for a community prayer service with a circular setting. Make sure there is a small table that can be used as an altar. You will also need five candles.

B. Ask for volunteers:
   (1) to prepare at least two songs: Glory to God in the Highest and a final hymn of their choice (praise or thanksgiving).
   (2) to bring candles to the altar after the first prayer.
   (3) to read the Scriptural Reading: Ecclesiastes 3:1-13

C Distribute copies of the prayer service to everyone. Begin music to allow everyone to be quiet and to be ready for the celebration of the onset of the new millennium.

Prayer:
   God of Life, we have arrived at this special moment of Kairos -
   a moment of grace, truth and decision.
   We recognize your precious gift of time -
   for conversion and hope.
   May we embrace this moment with gratitude
   And leave behind this darkness of evil -
   where self-interests, domination and injustice prevail.
   Grace us with your light as we welcome
   the beginnings of this new millennium.

Procession:
   The volunteers bring the five lighted candles to the altar. Each candle represents an aspect of the Jubilee:
   Let the Land Lie Fallow. Forgive Debt.
   Free Those in Slavery. Restore Just Relations.
   Celebrate.
   Announce each of the aspects as the candle is placed on the altar

Song of Praise:
   Glory to God in the highest
   And peace to God's people on earth.

Prayer for all:
   We thank you for gathering us together to celebrate this special moment.
   Open our hearts and minds that we may recognize the new paths and visions you have for us.
   Continue to bless each dawn with hope and joy. Amen.

Reading:
   Ecclesiastes 3:1-13

Reflection:
   In what ways do the teachings of our faith call us to be Jubilee people in the new millennium?

Moments of Silence:
   Call each person to silence. . . to a profound listening to God. . . to a silence that stirs and strengthens the heart and will.

Prayer for all:
   Living God, we pray for all peoples at the dawn of this new millennium:
   For those women shut off from a full life by tradition and practice.
   For those people who are oppressed and exploited.
   For those denied their freedom and dignity by systems and authorities.
   For those forced to leave their homelands because of their ideologies.
   For those seeking answers and meaning to their lives within their own cultures and religions.
   For those who labor too long and too hard only to barely feed and clothe themselves and their families.
   For those forced to sell their bodies to survive.
   For the land that we have abused and earth that we have misused.

For those women and men who live lives of
quiet desperation at the hands of the powerful
and prestigious.
For these and all who suffer.
We pray that governments may work in
collaboration and solidarity.
We pray in the spirit of this Jubilee, asking that
the Church may once again
Give joyful expression to Your creative love.
Which breaks down barriers and unites
persons to persons, women to men, communi-
ty to community and humanity to creation.
Which gives meaning and hope to empty lives
And makes us reach out to each other in
generous self-giving.
Which makes us more complete ourselves.
So God, fulfill your promise in us
For the sake of all human beings and creation
through Jesus Christ. Amen.

Blessing: (leader)

(With hands joined together, blessing is given)
Spirit of God - Holy God, Wind of God,
Fire of God, Life of God. . .
Anoint us to be a people of your Good News,
Make your justice, your work,
and your love real through our lives. Amen.

Final Prayer: (all)

Loving Creator,
We thank you for new beginnings and new
hopes.
Enable us to celebrate your Jubilee
with joy and gratitude, with love and mercy,
in loving service to one another.
Let us find ways to respect the earth and the
human dignity of all God's children through
letting the land lie fallow and forgiving debts.
This we ask through Jesus Christ,
Who came as brother and servant to us all.

A Celebration for Jubilee (for Eucharist Celebrations)

In coordination with a priest from your community, plan for a Mass that highlights this Jubilee spirit and celebration. Prepare appropriate songs for the Mass.

Divide into four small groups and make a banner, poster or symbol about Jubilee and display it in the church during the celebration of the Jubilee Mass.

Prayers and Readings Recommended for this Eucharistic Celebration:

Opening Words:

We give thanks as we gather today
and celebrate the continued grace of life
around us.
We stand in need of mercy and forgiveness
but with the faith and hope to mark a new
beginning
As we start a new millennium - a time for
jubilee.

Penitential Rite:

For the times we have simply conformed to the pattern of this world: preaching in your power of love while we succumb to the love of power, proclaiming your justice while we remain caught up in the structures of injustice. Lord have mercy.

For the many times we failed to witness to your all-embracing love: living in luxury where many suffer, starve and labor in vain, smothering the tenderness of men and the creative thinking of women. Christ have mercy.

For the times we refused to believe in your Word and trust in your providence: remaining silent and indifferent in the midst of abuse, surplus and exploitation, cowards in the face of opposition to truth and compassion. Lord, have mercy.

May the God of compassion have mercy on us, forgive us our sins and bring us to life everlasting.

Opening Prayer:

God of love and mercy, you call us to be your people, you gift us with your abundant grace. Make us a holy people, radiating the fullness of your love. Form us into a community, a people who care, expressing your compassion. Remind us day after day of our baptismal call to serve, with joy and courage. Teach us how to grow in wisdom and grace and joy in your presence. Through Jesus and in your Spirit, we make this prayer.

First Reading:

Leviticus 25:1-10

Responsorial Psalm:

(excerpts from Psalm 145)

Response:

O God, you are good to all and compassionate towards all your works.

I will extol you, O my God,
And I will praise your name forever.
Your greatness is unsearchable.
Generation after generation proclaims
your might.

They publish the fame of your abundant goodness
And joyfully sing of your justice.
O God, you are gracious and merciful,
Slow to anger and of great kindness.
You lift up all who are fallen
And raise up all who are bowed down.
The eyes of all look hopefully to you, you open your hand
And satisfy the desire of every living thing.

Gospel:

Luke 4:16-21 or Matthew 25:31-46

Prayers of the Faithful:

In deep trust and faith in our God, let us gather all our prayers and pray in humbleness: LORD, HEAR OUR PRAYER.

For the Churches throughout the world that the Spirit may move all to become a community of equals in the service of the poor. God, stir us into action, we pray.

For the leaders of the nations that they may establish and defend justice, equality and peace. God, give us your wisdom and righteousness, we pray.

For those who suffer oppression and violence that they may learn to speak out, unite in resistance and continue the struggle to overcome evil. God, move us to compassion and solidarity, we pray.

That the churches may minister together in the service of Christ as witnesses to our God of love. God, grant us right relation among all who call on your name, we pray.

For those intentions in the silence of our hearts, we pray.

Priest:

O Gracious and merciful God, you are indeed the source of all goodness and joy. Pour out your spirit on us that we forever trust in the power of your love through Christ our Lord.

Concluding Prayer:

Eternal God, creator and sustainer of life,
You grace each of us with equal measure in your love.
Let us learn to love our neighbors more deeply,
So that we can create peaceful and just communities.
Inspire us with the courage to proclaim the truth
And strength to work for justice and peace.
Impel us to use our creative energies
To build the structures we need,
To overcome the obstacles of intolerance and indifference.
Waken in us a spirit of joy
That we may celebrate all that is good and human
Especially as we rejoice in this Jubilee.
We ask this through Christ our Lord.

Blessing:

Go forth into the world in peace,
Looking up to Jesus, who was wounded for your transgressions,
And bearing about in your lives the love and joy and peace which are the marks of Jesus on his disciples; and so may the blessing of God, Father, Son and Holy Spirit be upon you.

Creating a Jubilee Banner

Reflection: Every human being and certainly every Christian has a social responsibility in this age of globalization; the present state of the world demands conversion. In the Jubilee context, conversion involves 'restoring' land, 'remitting' debts and 'freeing' slaves — which in today's terms means ecological and environmental care and protection, jobs and empowerment of the poor, elimination of poverty, and promotion of radical and much needed social changes. There is no point in celebrating a Jubilee unless we are aware of the evils it is supposed to remedy. Today, it is not just that isolated aspects of the world are evil or that individual countries are going through hard times. God's creation as a whole is affected.

Our world embodies neither the ideal God had when he created it for all, nor God's vision for its future in which all would work and enjoy the fruits of their labor. Indeed, not only does the world not embody this ideal and this vision, it denies them to the majority of the human race. Thus, what is evil

is the widespread poverty and the fact that poor people are always condemned to the slow death induced by the present world order. To become converted to the truth, to see things as they are in themselves and recognize their causes, to act on what we have seen, is the most important thing the world demands of us. Daunted though we may be at the sight of the world we have built that is nevertheless where we must start, if we do not start here, we will not be able to hear the good news of Jubilee and celebrate this Jubilee as we ought to.

With your group: Have everyone share their ideas for Jubilee symbols that could be used on a Jubilee banner. Are there any similarities? How can you design a banner that captures the spirit of everyone in the group? What symbols would be most appropriate? What kinds of colors? What shapes, sizes would be appropriate? What kinds of art skills can group participants contribute? Draw a final design for your banner. If time permits, start construction on the banner. If not, plan for a time when it can be constructed.

Celebrating Signs of Hope in Developing Countries

The celebration of Jubilee is a commitment to justice for all people. Gathering together in the year 2000 to celebrate signs of hope in developing countries, to celebrate our kinship with our brothers and sisters in these countries, and to learn how we can grow in solidarity with them are all ways to create a Jubilee world where we share social responsibility for the global common good.

With your group, go through the following suggestions and explore some possible options in developing a celebration of solidarity; you may choose to put a planning committee together to reflect at a later date on your initial discussions and then to set a specific agenda with dates and assigned tasks. Your group may decide to pull together only one celebration and then evaluate the results before planning subsequent ones.

1. Discuss what countries in Africa, Latin America, and Asia you wish to learn about, pray for, and support in some way. Have the participants share what they know—or do not know—about developing regions and/or specific countries and discuss why such knowledge is important in this age of globalization, in the context of Church's teachings. You may decide to simply identify regions and do more research before you choose specific countries.

2. Look at the following suggested elements of a celebration. Discuss how they can be combined to allow your group/class to grow in understanding so you can develop the solidarity our Faith calls us to.

a. Information sharing: Call local colleges, churches, mission groups, refugee groups, diocesan peace and justice offices, etc. to see if someone from a specific country, or someone who has worked in that country, can come and speak to your group. Some mission organizations, such as Maryknoll, have videos and/or printed material available on the countries in which they serve (see Resources for contact information). Research in libraries and on the Internet to find facts about the country—the people and their way of life, issues of education, health, gender equity, poverty, conflicts, debt problems, etc. Assign group members a specific issue and prepare presentations and/or brief handouts and/or posters on these issues.

Be sure to identify some signs of hope in these countries and in the work of groups and organizations that are working in solidarity with the people in these countries; again, mission organizations can be a resource. It is also important to look for the ways that we are connected to poorer countries in a global economy. Explore how the choices and policies we make in this country may affect citizens in other countries, especially the poor and marginalized (see the newsletter on social responsibility in the age of globalization that accompanied the materials for this Jubilee and Justice workshop).

b. Advocacy suggestions: through the possible contacts and research noted above, identify some ways to be a part of the signs of hope for the women, men and children in the country on which you focus.

c. Prayer: Discuss the appropriate role of prayer in your celebration and in how prayer can extend your solidarity with other members of our global family. Consider a prayer group that meets regularly to pray for those suffering around the world.

e. Culture: Can you offer snacks or a meal (depending on the time of the meeting) based on recipes from the country and/or using foods from the country? Is there a source for tapes and CDs from different countries in your area? (If you live in an area where there are immigrants and refugees from Hispanic, African or Asian countries, music tapes are often available in stores that serve that specific immigrant community. See the resource listings for mail order international tapes.) Can you locate pictures of local scenes and the different population groups in the country? If you have a guest from the country, ask that s/he wear or bring clothes that have cultural significance.

How would organizing a celebration based on the elements above help your group members nurture their own spiritual development and at the same time develop their understanding of social responsibility in an age when there are increasing links between all members of the global community?

Suggestions for Action

1. There is need to keep the hope going, especially as times can be difficult and discouragement can easily set in. Aim to share with someone or some group a token/poem/song etc. of hope at least once every month (be specific about your date: every first Monday of the month, etc.).

2. Make a difference even in your own homes: have a weekly session during 2000 that includes reflection on the Jubilee values we are called to live and on how these values can be reflected as much as possible: care for the environment, more time for your family, participation in community activities, etc.

3. Plan a monthly Jubilee celebration during 2000 in your home and/or school and/or parish to focus on justice in the new millennium.

Resources

Maryknoll Office for Global Concerns
P.O Box 29132
Washington, DC 20017
Tel: (202) 832-1780
Fax: (202) 832-5195
E-mail: mknolldc@igc.org

U.S. Catholic Mission Association
3029 4th St. NE
Washington, DC 20017-1102
Tel: (202) 832-3112
Fax: (202) 832-3688
E-mail: uscma@igc.org

House of Musical Traditions (for world music)
7040 Carroll Avenue
Takoma Park, MD 20912
Tel: (301) 270-9090

We are human beings together. And if Jesus and the Mystical Body of
Christ means anything, it is that they are networked together. If we are
going to survive, we have to learn that.

Sister Helen Prejean

Do not let a day pass in the new millennium without an act that contributes to justice for all.